P9-CRP-940

The Story of Moody Church

The Story
of Moody Church

by

Robert G. Flood

MOODY PRESS

CHICAGO

© 1985 by
THE MOODY BIBLE INSTITUTE
OF CHICAGO

Library of Congress Cataloging-in-Publication Data

Flood, Robert G.
 The story of Moody Church.

   1. Moody Memorial Church (Chicago, Ill.) — History.
2. Chicago (Ill.) — Church history.   I. Title.
BX9999.C46F56   1985   280'.4'0977311   85-21776
ISBN 0-8024-0339-5
ISBN 0-8024-0539-8 (pbk.)

   1 2 3 4 5 6 7 Printing/RR/Year 88 87 86 85

Printed in the United States of America

Acknowledgements

A special word of thanks to all those who assisted me in gathering material for this history, including Pastor Erwin Lutzer, Associate Pastor Bruce Jones, church historian Carl Johnson, Charles Hayward, and Evelyn Rankin. Tribute also to Ralph Munroe, who provided printouts from the word processor.

73980

Contents

Introduction

The Moody Memorial Church stands like a giant brick bulwark in the heart of Chicago's near North Side. For more than a century it has been the hub of the city's evangelicalism.

Its beginnings are intertwined with the history of Chicago and the history of its illustrious founder, Dwight L. Moody. Near the church are reminders of the past. A statue of Abraham Lincoln, who once visited Dwight L. Moody's Sunday school, stands a few hundred yards northeast of the church in adjacent Lincoln Park. And directly across the street from the church's main entrance, the Chicago Historical Society preserves the story of the city's passing years.

Evidence of the "new" Chicago is nearby too. Residents of Carl Sandburg Village with its vast, modern complex of high-rise apartments, can look down onto the church. The hundred-story John Hancock Center towers to the southeast. The upper end of Michigan Avenue's "Magnificent Mile" is less than a five-minute jog away. Rush Street nightlife shouts for attention just to the southeast, and tourists wander through Old Town two blocks west.

The Moody Church has one of the richest heritages of any church in the United States—or the world. It has produced missionaries like William Borden of Yale and Fredrik Franson, who founded what is today The Evangelical Alliance Mission (TEAM), and a parade of others who have followed in their train. Because it has sent out hundreds of missionaries, Moody Church is known around the world.

With its 4,000-seat auditorium (and total capacity for around 7,500 when other rooms of the building are added), Moody Church has long hosted major events of the Christian community from world missions conferences and national Sunday school conventions to classical concerts and multi-night evangelistic crusades.

Over the years a literal parade of "Who's Who" in evangelicalism, from the United States and abroad, have preached from her pulpit. The funeral of evangelist Billy Sunday was held in Moody Church.

Moody Church has given Christianity literally scores of hymns and gospel songs. Along with those of Ira Sankey, who was Dwight L. Moody's famed soloist and songleader, they have come from the pens of D. B. Towner ("Trust and Obey," "My Anchor Holds," "Grace Greater Than Our Sin"), Harry Dixon Loes ("Blessed Redeemer," "All Things in Jesus,"), James M. Gray ("Only a Sinner"), and T. J. Bittikofer ("Complete in Thee"), all of whom belonged to Moody Church, served as organist, or perhaps led its choirs.

Not all of the church's musicians are figures of the distant past, though. Avis B. Christiansen, who went to be with the Lord as recently as January 1985, had joined Moody Church in 1915. In 1920 she wrote the words to "Blessed Redeemer" and the next year "Love Found a Way." Her hymns are known worldwide for many of her delightful lyrics have been translated into various languages.

Merrill Dunlop, long owner of his own music publishing firm and still active on the Bible conference circuit, wrote the music to "Only One Life" and "He Was Wounded for Our Transgressions" and both words and music to "My Sins Are Blotted Out, I Know."

If you worship this Sunday in one of the churches of America, you may well sing songs written or composed by the people of Moody Church.

Some of the church's heritage, of course, is linked to its proximity to the Moody Bible Institute, one mile south on LaSalle Drive. The old Moody Church stood at Chicago and LaSalle from 1873 to 1928 and served as the school's auditorium until as late as 1939. The Institute's current president, George Sweeting, pastored Moody Church from 1966 to 1971. The relationship has always been a warm one, but though the two organizations have a common founder, they have never been organizationally tied.

Moody Church still stands at the crossroads of America, reaching out both near and far. Its late night radio program, "Songs in the Night," for example, is heard on more than two hundred stations, from Alaska to the Caribbean.

No book of this length can do more than give an overview. But may it be enough to document the impact of the Moody Memorial Church in history, its outreach today, and its potential even yet as "the church that can change the city in a city that could change the world."

1

Dwight L. Moody: Founder

The sound of the woodchopper's ax echoed through the trees in North-field, a village in northwest Massachusetts within sight of New Hamp-shire and Vermont. The young boy swinging the ax abounded with energy.

His name was Dwight Lyman Moody.

The boy knew how to work. It took that kind of person to survive on those rocky New England farms. Concerning that region, someone once quipped, "There are sufficient stones to build four fences to the acre."

Moody was related to Jonathan Edwards, Harriet Beecher Stowe, Oliver Wendell Holmes, Presidents Grover Cleveland and Franklin Roosevelt. But there was little to suggest in Moody's boyhood days that he too would become a man of fame.

When Moody was still young, his father died, leaving him with six brothers and two sisters. The oldest of the boys ran away. The broken-hearted widow, doubly bereft, began an unaccredited but heroic struggle against unrelenting poverty.

At seventeen Moody traveled across the state to Boston, where he went to work in his uncle's shoe store.

Moody turned out to be a first class salesman. No shoddy pair of shoes walked past him without a challenge. Nor was he content to let his pros-pects come to him. He stood out on the sidewalks and went after the crowds. He believed you had to go where the people were—a conviction that carried over into his career as an evangelist.

In Boston, persuaded by his uncle, Moody began to attend Mount Vernon Congregational church. There he sat in a Bible class headed by

Edward Kimball, a man who followed up his pupils. Concerned about Moody's soul and his conversion, Kimball hastened down to the shoe store one day and got right to the point. Jesus had died for him, Kimball pressed, and it was time for Moody to make a decision. The timing was right. Moody responded.

Then just as suddenly as he had left the hamlet of Northfield for Boston, Moody impulsively left Boston for Chicago, not telling his family. He hopped an immigration train, which cost $5 for the three-day trip. Upon his arrival in Chicago in the fall of 1856, he dashed off a quick note to his family, including the startling information that "God is the same here as in Boston."

A boot store hired Moody and made him its traveling representative. Without the aid of today's outpour of self-help books, the ambitious Moody immediately set his goal: a fortune of $100,000.

But shoes were no longer his only product. He now told people about the Lord. Moody rented a pew in Plymouth Church and went to the streets to fill it. He not only filled one pew, but four. He did not "pick and choose" his prospects. Everyone from beggars to business executives were eligible for a Moody approach:

"Are you a Christian?"

Unless the prospect could promptly retort with a convincing answer, he would find Moody in quick pursuit.

"Why not?"

Moody's straightforward approach took courage. The streets were tough. Corruption flourished, and temptations abounded. But Moody let nothing swerve him from his mission.

When he asked to teach a Bible class, Moody was told there was nothing open. That did not stop him. He went out on the streets and recruited his own class. They were urchins of all sorts, but he welcomed whomever he found.

Moody could just as well relate to the man of means and to those in the top ranks of Chicago's social class. God is no respecter of persons, and Moody took men as they were.

For a time Moody rode the streets on an Indian pony, rounding up children for his Sunday school and handing out candy apples. Some critics no doubt wrote it off as a publicity stunt. But if Moody wanted to draw attention to himself, it was only because he wanted to point all he could to the Savior.

As the work grew, Moody searched for larger quarters. In a section of Chicago known as "Little Hell," he rented a large, grimy beer hall on North Market Street and filled it with more than five hundred on Sundays. Before long, word of Moody's success in the inner city reached Abraham Lincoln. It was hardly a place where you would want to host a dignitary; nevertheless, the president-elect dropped in to see it for himself on his way from Springfield to Washington, D.C., for his first inauguration.

As he was leaving, Lincoln told the children, "With close attention to your teachers and the hard work to put into practice what you learn from them, some of you may also become President of the United States, like myself, as you have had better opportunities than I have had."

Moody proved to be the primary catalyst for a movement that soon became known as the Young Men's Christian Association (YMCA), of which for a time he was president. The rise of the movement in Great Britain, as well as an eventual parallel organization, the YWCA, are also attributed to D. L. Moody.

By 1860 Moody was making a major impact on Chicago. But the winds of war were blowing. Moody was an abolitionist and supported the Union, but he could not bear to "shoot down a fellow human being." So in Chicago he conducted missionary services among the Union soldiers at Camp Douglas and later, after the camp had been converted into a war prison, among some nine thousand Confederate prisoners.

It was always Moody's bent to go where the people were. But most of the soldiers were on the front lines, not in Chicago. Moody offered himself as a volunteer chaplain and headed South—to Shiloh, Murfreesboro, Chattanooga. He was among the first to enter Richmond and visited the Civil War battlefront nine different times.

He used the boom of his voice instead of a cannon to mount his spiritual assault. The Bible was his ammunition.

During the war, Moody fell in love and in 1862 married Emma Revell, sister of Fleming H. Revell, a name still prominent today in the Christian publishing world. Though Emma was only fifteen at the time, Moody had found a partner entirely in tune with the call of God upon his life, one whom he saw as the "divinely appointed balance wheel of his existence."

Back in Chicago after the Civil War, two movements took much of his attention: the YMCA and the spread of the Sunday school throughout the Midwest. On the former, he worked closely with Chicago merchant John V. Farwell and raised money to build the first "Y" hall in America. Cyrus McCormick, inventor of the reaper, gave Moody the first $10,000 for the project. It burned four months later, but before the embers had cooled, he had agents out raising funds to replace it.

Moody knew how to tap the well-to-do for funds, not for his own welfare but for the welfare of others and the advance of the gospel. By then, Moody had shifted his priorities and scuttled his ambition for personal wealth. He could have become a millionaire, said his close friends, but the Wall Street panic of 1857 convinced him he should not regard faith as primarily "an aid to fortune." Of his merchant associates in Chicago, Moody once said, "I felt I could equal any of them, except one—and that one was Marshall Field."

In 1860, at age twenty-three, Moody was earning $5000 a year—big money in those days. His first year full time in Christian work, his income shriveled to $150.

As the number of Moody's converts grew, he realized he would have to build an edifice where spiritual growth could be nourished. So in 1864, with twelve charter members, Moody opened the Illinois Street Independent Church, having an auditorium seating 1,500. The church called J. H. Harwood as its pastor, and Moody served as one of the deacons.

This event marked the birth of what is today Moody Church.

One year later Chicago was already the world's busiest railroad center and the nation's largest grain shipper. "Chicago is a lively city," said Moody. "Much more so than Boston."

The crowds grew at his church, and the Lord prospered.

Then came tragedy.

On an October Sunday in 1871, as Moody was holding one of his regular evening services, ominous flames erupted on Chicago's South Side. The story of Mrs. O'Leary's cow stands as only legend, but whatever may have sparked the initial blaze, by midnight the entire populace was fleeing in panic. The inferno swept northward block by block, reducing the city to ashes.

Dwight and Emma dispatched their two children to the suburbs with a neighbor, gathered up a few belongings, and fled.

The great Chicago fire destroyed Moody's home, a lovely building that had been completely furnished and provided by friends less than a year earlier. The harrowing experience turned Mrs. Moody, then twenty-eight, gray almost overnight.

The fire destroyed the YMCA and Moody's church. Yet in Moody's eyes it was not the worst catastrophe that could happen to man. Far worse was it that anyone should not hear clearly the gospel. The Chicago fire impressed upon Moody a new urgency. With his typical endless energy, he again sprang into action. He rebuilt within a few weeks, named his new building the North Side Tabernacle, and turned it into a relief center to help feed and clothe the thousands who had lost their homes in the fire.

Moody would soon take the gospel to Great Britain. With him would go his soloist, Ira Sankey, a former internal revenue agent whom he had recruited at a Christian convention in Indianapolis. The combination of the short, bearded evangelist and the tall, side-whiskered Sankey proved a spectacular success. Their first British Isles campaign started slowly. Little seemed to happen at first—at least on the surface. Britons were not used to Moody's informal style of preaching or to Sankey's portable organ. They winced at the American evangelist's accent and his occasional poor English, but the Spirit of God began to work.

The campaign extended into weeks, then months. Stores by the thousands displayed revival posters. Government leaders, including British Prime Minister William Gladstone, complimented and endorsed Moody. Communists denounced his work as a "bourgeois plot to import intellectual opium."

Moody and Sankey moved on to Scotland. Revival soon took hold. Moody drew tremendous gatherings in Glasgow. When an auditorium overflowed, he addressed an estimated 50,000 outside from a buggy. The pair moved on to Ireland, touching Belfast, then tackled London itself. That turned out to be his greatest triumph. Months later his crowds had exceeded 2.5 million.

Soon Moody-Sankey hymnals were selling briskly—both in Great Britain and America. Royalties began to mount, leading to rumors that Moody and Sankey were growing rich on them and that Barnum, the circus magnate, was backing them. It was the kind of story that often plagues even the most reputable evangelist.

Moody sent the first British royalties, totaling $35,000, back home to Chicago to complete his newest church structure—at Chicago Avenue and LaSalle. By the turn of the century the hymnal had generated well over $1 million in royalties, but it was all channeled into evangelistic and philanthropic causes. Moody and Sankey themselves made not a penny of personal profit from the hymnals.

Neither did Moody and Sankey let the success of the British Isles campaign spoil them. They clearly understood the source of the spiritual power that had swept Great Britain. And if it could happen there, it could also happen in America. Moody began to outline an American revival. The nation needed it. The Civil War, like all wars, had disrupted social morality. People chased after easy wealth. Corruption penetrated high political office.

Target cities were New York, Brooklyn, and Philadelphia—with Brooklyn the opener in October 1875. Poor and rich alike poured in, though the press gave mixed reviews. Some once more ridiculed Moody's grammar. On that point the *New York Tribune* came to Moody's defense. "Christianity," said the paper, "is not a matter of grammar." And thousands came to the Lord.

It was a similar story in Philadelphia, where merchant John Wanamaker let Moody use as a hall the old freight depot of the Pennsylvania Railroad, which Wanamaker had just purchased and which he later made into a store. At Philadelphia one evening, President Grant and several of his cabinet sat on the platform.

And so on to New York. Again, great welcomes, tremendous crowds, and an outpouring of God's salvation.

There followed campaigns in Chicago, Boston, Baltimore, Cleveland, Cincinnati, Richmond, Denver, Colorado Springs, St. Louis, San Francisco. With more time he could have also gone to Canada and Mexico. They wanted him.

If those who turned out for Moody expected to hear a man of polished eloquence, they were disappointed. Yet Moody could communicate superbly. He was in tune with the common man, and he was also in tune with God. "He knew only two books," Henry Drummond once said, "the Bible and Human Nature. Out of these he spoke; and because both are books of life, his words were afire with life; and the people to whom he spoke, being real people, listened and understood."

Moody treated the Bible as a living book. He knew it not so much as a scholar but almost by intuition. Its historic characters were his personal friends or enemies. They were not misty outlines of legendary lore. Wrote one observer of Moody's day, "He touches them and they live, move and meet you face to face."

Wrote John H. Elliott, "Mr. Moody impressed me tremendously by his sort of restrained force that made his words come out red-hot and without affectation. You didn't smell sulphur and brimstone in his sermon. He just talked to his flock on the common sins and urged them to turn away from them. He did not intone or shout, nor did he gesture much; but every movement counted for something worthwhile."

In a tribute to Moody at the time of his death in 1899, the *Chicago Times Herald* wrote:

> Moody found that the sacrificial atonement of the Nazarene had power to touch the hearts of men, and he preached it as Paul preached it in Syria and Macedonia, without embellishment or studied rhetoric. He drew not upon archaeology or cryptograms, but upon the human heart, the daily life, for his proofs of the doctrines of redemption and immortality.
>
> He left the battle of the creeds to be waged by the cloistered scholars. His profession was not theology. He was about his Master's business. While theologians emptied pews with dogmatic controversy, Moody filled great auditoriums with the masses of the people who were hungry for the simple consolations of religion.

P. W. Philpott, former pastor of Moody Memorial Church, wrote in the *Chicago Tribune*, "Moody's three triumphant tours of Great Britain had a tremendous influence in drawing England and America closer together."

A second American campaign followed—and that would only build momentum for an era of crusades across the nation that would span almost another two decades—before Moody's death in Kansas City in 1899.

When Moody's life on earth ended, America, Europe, even the world mourned, though it was a godly sorrow. God had used him to change millions of lives and to leave a spiritual legacy that continues to impact the world to this very hour. The stocky man with broad shoulders left his indelible imprint upon Carl Sandburg's "city of broad shoulders," where he founded both the Moody Bible Institute and Moody Church. Chicago at one time claimed this mighty preacher, but by the time he died the world claimed him.

"Never has a man made more of his talents than did D. L. Moody," wrote Philpott.

"Lacking eloquence and with an unimposing platform presence, he became the greatest preacher of the age.

"Meagerly educated himself, he rose to be one of America's foremost educators.

"Knowing little of business, he developed into a great executive successfully administering a gigantic project." (To the original board of Moody Bible Institute, which he founded in 1886, Moody appointed such men as Cyrus H. McCormick, Jr., son of the inventor of the reaper; T. W. Harvey, retail lumber giant and founder of the town of Harvey south of Chicago; Nathaniel S. Bouton, Chicago's Superintendent of Public Works; and Robert S. Scott, senior partner in what is now Carson, Pirie, Scott and Co.).

"Born in poverty and dying a poor man," observed Philpott, Moody's philanthropy "mounted into the millions."

On a chilly day in December 1899, just before the turn of the century, they buried D. L. Moody on the top of a round knoll only a couple of hundred yards from his Northfield birthplace. But in those intervening sixty-five years upon earth, Moody had traveled a million miles for the sake of his Savior and preached to 100 million people.

The world, ever since, has never been quite the same.*

*Publisher's note: Adapted from the book, *Teaching the Word Reaching the World,* by Robert G. Flood and Jerry B. Jenkins, released in 1985 by Moody Press in celebration of Moody Bible Institute's 1986 Centennial.©1985 by Moody Bible Institute.

2

The First Fifty Years
(1864-1914)

Civil war raged in distant states to Chicago's southeast. Three years earlier, in 1860, President-elect Abraham Lincoln had visited Dwight L. Moody's Sunday school on his way through Chicago to occupy the White House. Now as armies of the North and South clashed across the Potomac from Washington, D.C., Lincoln called a national day of "fasting, humiliation and prayer."

"It is the duty of nations as well as of men," he said,

> to own their dependence upon the overruling power of God, to confess their sins and transgressions, in humble sorrow, yet with assured hope that genuine repentance will lead to mercy and pardon. . . .
>
> We have been the recipients of the choicest bounties of Heaven. We have been preserved, these many years, in peace and prosperity. We have grown in numbers, wealth and power, as no other nation has ever grown. But we have forgotten God.

While from the nation's capital the President called for national repentance, Dwight L. Moody to the west in Chicago confronted his city's citizens with the gospel of personal repentance and reminded his audiences that many had "forgotten God."

Converts increased, and it became a serious question what to do with them. Moody tried to get them to join existing churches, but the poorer classes felt strange and out of place in beautiful edifices. Moreover, the rough and ready methods of Moody suited them better than the more deliberate proceedings of the ordinary church service. Most converts had no previous religious connections and therefore no preference for one denomination rather than another.

It was inevitable: if Moody could not find the right church for them, he would have to build one of his own. So he did—in 1864—the Illinois Street Mission, or church, located on the south side of Illinois Street between Wells and LaSalle.

That event was the official birth of what today is Moody Memorial Church.

The Illinois Street church held 1,500 people in its main hall and also contained several classrooms. It was dedicated early in 1864 and soon became one of the most thriving and active churches in the city. The church building was in almost constant use, and Moody was the life and moving spirit of all.

Moody himself, however, never pastored the church. He was only one of its deacons. Nor was Moody ever ordained, though many denominations offered to ordain him. Moody declined. He did not want to be bound by denominationalism in general, let alone a particular one. He preferred to be independent, free to do things his own way, an evangelist to the church at large.

Moody's Sunday school had taken possession of the new building on Sunday, February 24, 1864. Ten months later, on Christmas Eve, the Illinois Street Independent Church was officially organized with just twelve members.

In 1866 the church called its first pastor, J. H. Harwood. After three years, Harwood left to take up pioneer work in Missouri and later in California. Harwood eventually organized more than fifty churches and three Christian colleges.

When the Illinois Street Church burned in the great Chicago fire of 1871, Moody appealed to his business friends for funds to rebuild. Only eleven weeks later, the congregation dedicated a new temporary building at Wells and Ontario streets, called the "North Side Tabernacle." It served as both church and relief center to help feed and clothe the thousands who had lost their homes in the fire. Moody himself took up residence in the tabernacle for a time and spent his mornings scouting for neighborhood refugees.

Like the Illinois Street Church, it too was dedicated on Christmas Eve. When Moody returned from an East Coast fund-raising trip for the ceremonies, only a few rough shanties had yet arisen in the area—usually on the sheltered side of blackened, crumbling walls. Streets were blocked with rubbish. Holes gaped where homes and businesses had been.

The temporary structure served well for two years. Within a year after the fire, Chicago passed an ordinance outlawing wooden buildings in the downtown area. At the time of the fire, the city had 60,000 buildings, 40,000 constructed entirely of wood. Fifty miles of streets had been paved with wood blocks.

God prospered the North Side Tabernacle, and the congregation soon had to relocate. Moody appealed for contributions, however small. Sunday school children gave their pennies. By the spring of 1873 the church had purchased a lot on the northwest corner of Chicago and LaSalle for $22,500. Today it is the site of Moody Bible Institute's women's dormitory (Houghton Hall) and Moody Bookstore, and one of modern Chicago's busiest intersections.

Construction on the site began just as Moody and Sankey were leaving for what would become their first great campaign abroad. The church's first story was completed in Moody's absence, and the church opened for services on New Year's Eve, 1873. That was a year of financial depression, and construction of upper levels had to be delayed. It was June 1876 before "The Chicago Avenue Church" was completed and dedicated—and then only with the help of royalties from the Moody and Sankey Hymnbook. When the next year Chicago installed its first telephones, Moody-Sankey campaign hymns were among the most popular songs used to demonstrate the new invention.

Louis H. Sullivan, Chicago's renowned architect, painted the interior of the new Moody Church with a most unusual fresco design—a botanical motif of leaves and flowers. Chicago newspapers gave the work rave reviews, calling it both "scientific and artistic," "warm and cheerful," and a "significant contribution to the art culture and taste of the west." By and large, the congregation itself thought the fresco was horrible. It was finally painted over.

Bible scholar William J. Erdman served as the first pastor of the Chicago Avenue Church, from 1876 to 1878. Charles M. Morton followed for one year, then George C. Needham for two. Both of these young men had been in the work at the Illinois Street Church, where they were well-grounded in evangelism. The church went without a regular pastor from 1881 to 1885, but the work prospered anyway, for it was of God, not man. Charles F. Goss pastored from 1885 to 1890.

During these years Moody founded what would become Moody Bible Institute. Although Moody Church and Moody Bible Institute have never been organizationally affiliated, it was the Chicago Avenue church site that, at least indirectly, determined the site of Moody Bible Institute.

The story is well known. One evening John Morrison, an usher in the Chicago Avenue Church, stepped outside the church's northwest door for a breath of air.

"Is that you, Morrison?" asked Moody, who was to preach that night. "Do you see that lot? Let us pray the Lord to give it to us for a school."

The two men knelt and prayed right there.

In their wildest imaginations, those two could not have envisioned how God would answer that prayer, nor the vast complex that would stand on that very lot and the surrounding properties a century later.

During the 1880s Charles Blanchard, president of Wheaton College, supplied the Chicago Avenue Church pulpit for a year and a half, and in these years he also assisted greatly in securing the monies to start Moody's Bible school on the properties adjacent to the church.

In 1878 Moody Church commissioned from its own ranks its first missionary, Fredrik Franson, who went to the fields of Europe with such impassioned zeal that he was dubbed "the gunpowder preacher." Wherever he went, it seemed, he stirred either a revival or a riot.

Standing in the open plaza of an Armenian town, Franson tried to preach to the crowd surrounding him. Knowing only a few Armenian words, he was greatly handicapped. But the earnest expression on his face, down which tears were streaming, and his hands pointed heavenward spoke more eloquently than words the message of God's love. Hearts throughout the audience melted, and conviction of sin swept over the multitude. A revival started that resulted in the salvation of thousands of souls.

At other times, Franson drew fierce opposition. Once while kneeling in prayer in an Armenian church, he was surrounded by a half dozen women, who punctuated the insults they heaped on him by spitting in his face. Franson was forced out of a town in Norway by a mob who yelled invectives at him as a preacher of hellfire. On the outskirts he turned, faced the mob, and said, with prophetic vision, "As I am now driven out of this town, so you will be driven out in a future day." His prophecy was fulfilled twenty years later when a fire destroyed almost the entire town.

Franson kindled revival fires not only in Europe but also in New Zealand, where he organized in 1902 one of that nation's first evangelical churches. Franson personally recruited some one hundred missionaries for Hudson Taylor's China. In 1890 he founded the Scandinavian Alliance Mission, which in 1949 became The Evangelical Alliance Mission (TEAM), today one of the world's largest. Franson was a lifelong member of Moody Church. When he died in 1908, great crowds, including some of his converts worldwide, gathered for his burial in Chicago's Mount Olive Cemetery.

Moody Church produced other missionary legends of their time—among them William Whiting Borden, who became known as "Borden of Yale." Borden's mother lived on Chicago's "Gold Coast" and transfered her membership to nearby Moody Church after an experience of spiritual renewal, bringing son Billy with her. There the boy invited Jesus Christ into his life at age seven.

Though born into wealth and privilege, Borden's burden for world missions during his college days at Yale and the spiritual example of his life on campus made such impact that many other students were prompted to pursue careers on the mission field—particularly in China and India. Borden himself died suddenly in Egypt of spinal meningitis, while enroute to China. Still his influence continued to spread.

In the last days of his life Borden gave $1 million to the cause of missions, including $100,000 to Moody Church so that it could take advantage of its downtown setting to preach the gospel to a teeming city of thirty different nationalities. Though ordained in Moody Church, Borden modestly turned down all invitations to preach from its pulpit. For many years a large photo of Borden hung on the north wall of the church's Woolley Hall history center.

Herbert Hudson Taylor, son of the founder of the China Inland Mission, was also a member of Moody Church and one of its long-supported missionaries.

By 1890, Chicago had become the second largest city in the United States, with a population of more than 1 million. Of these, 80 percent were European immigrants or their children. The city raced on towards the close of the century and the excitement of its 1893 World's Fair. The Columbian Exposition drew some 27 million visitors from around the globe to the fair's 633 acres of gleaming white buildings. It was estimated that a visitor needed three weeks and would have to walk about 150 miles just to get a quick glance at all of the fair.

Dwight Moody quickly saw the fair's potential for outreach. In a great effort he mobilized Moody Bible Institute and more than eighty churches of Chicago, including the Moody Church, for an evangelistic thrust that brought nearly 2 million fairgoers face to face with the gospel.

The next year, Yale-educated Reuben A. Torrey, who had become superintendent of the Institute, was called as pastor of Moody Church. He continued in both positions until 1906—more than a decade later.

Though raised in a godly home, Torrey had by college days acquired only a veneer of Christianity. At Yale he buckled under social pressure and became a heavy drinker. In his senior year, however, he found personal salvation. When Moody came to town, Torrey involved himself in the crusade.

Torrey's conversion, however, had not settled all his intellectual doubts—even as he pursued theological studies at Yale Seminary. "The professors ... were all orthodox," Torrey later said, "but I was not."

Could he really believe in the resurrection, as told in the Scriptures? Torrey dug into the evidence in depth and found it overwhelming. "That conclusion," he said, "carried everything with it that was essential."

But Torrey had also followed the transcendental thinkers and read heavily in Unitarianism. Questions remained. From Yale, Torrey pursued studies in Leipzig and Erlangen, Germany, and faced head-on the arguments of the "higher critics." Abroad he settled the question once and for all. Yes, he could trust the Bible, its infallibility, its full authority. And he knew why. Torrey never wavered again.

On return from Germany, Torrey became superintendent of the city mission in Minneapolis. He gave up his salary and deliberately put himself out on a financial limb. City work gave him further seasoning and exposed him to the gospel's power in the lives of men. Such background produced a man who could handle himself and the Scriptures well, whether on skid row or among theological scholars. Said one biographer, "He could kneel beside a drunk in a mission or explain the gospel at an elegant dinner table."

The Chicago Avenue Church reeled in shock when Dwight Moody died suddenly during a December evangelistic crusade in Kansas City, just a few days before the turn of the twentieth century. Shortly after, the Chicago Evangelization Society, which Moody had founded, officially became Moody Bible Institute, and the Chicago Avenue Church was renamed The Moody Church.

During the closing years of his pastorate, Torrey was away much of the time in worldwide evangelistic work, so Moody Church hired its first assistant pastor, W. S. Jacoby. The crusades of R. A. Torrey, with Charles Alexander as his soloist, ultimately brought millions under the sound of the gospel during his career—with his impact upon Australia perhaps as great as upon any continent. In 1912, Torrey became dean of the Bible Institute of Los Angeles (now Biola University), where he served until 1924. When he died in 1928, he had written more than forty books, some of them still in print.

A. C. Dixon followed Torrey and pastored Moody Church from 1906 to 1911, coming from the well-known Ruggles Street Church in Boston. Dixon excelled in personal and public evangelism. He wrote a weekly two-column evangelistic appeal in the *Chicago Daily News,* held occasional noon-day theater meetings in the heart of the Loop that were attended by thousands, and assembled great Watch Night meetings, the largest of which, in 1908, packed Chicago's Coliseum with 12,000 people, while many were turned away. The church took advantage of the industrial distress of 1907-1908 and fed daily, both physically and spiritually, more than a thousand unemployed men for a period of two months or more.

Dixon also organized the Testimony Publishing Company, through which some 3 million copies of a 128-page book known as *The Fundamentals* were distributed free to Christian leaders throughout the world. Dixon resigned Moody Church in 1911 to pastor the historic Metropolitan Tabernacle in London, made famous by Charles Spurgeon. Eight years later he returned to the United States to pastor the University Baptist Church of Baltimore. He died in 1925.

E. W. Woolley, who had become assistant pastor under Dixon, served Moody Church as acting pastor from 1911 to 1915. Over several decades liberal theology had invaded many of America's churches, and naive clergymen offered parishoners a kingdom on earth that, they envisioned, would get better and better. In 1914, with the world on the brink of World War I, Moody Bible Institute sponsored a landmark Prophetic Bible Conference at Moody Church to reaffirm the doctrines of historic Christianity, both for the church at large and for the Institute itself. Ministers gathered from across America for the event.

Although newspapers that week criticized the conference for what it saw as a pessimistic tone, the ominous events of the world at that time, observed the late Dr. Wilbur M. Smith, "compelled journalists to resort to the very apocalyptic vocabulary that they decried."

That very year World War I erupted—just fifty years after the birth of Moody Church in 1864. The congregation, aware that temporal events can never change God's transcending powers or purposes, pressed forward in its unchanging mission.

3

Paul Rader: The Sawdust Years (1915-1922)

Dwight L. Moody opened his 1892 campaign in Denver.

Paul Rader, son of a devout Methodist preacher, was delighted.

When Rader's father had entertained famed evangelist Sam Jones in their parsonage home, Jones told little Paul that the greatest preacher in all the world was D. L. Moody and if he ever had a chance to hear him to be sure to do so.

Tickets had been handed out for the campaign, but Paul failed to get one. He made his way to the site of the meetings and tried to get in, but the large building was packed. So Paul went to the back of the building where stood a short, heavyset, and strongly built man who was pounding on the back door. Said the man, "What do you want, boy?"

"I want to get in to hear Mr. Moody preach," said Paul.

"Why do you want to hear Mr. Moody preach?" said the man.

"Because Sam Jones told me to."

"What did Sam Jones tell you?"

"He told me that Mr. Moody was the best preacher in the world, and I haven't got a ticket to hear him."

Said the little heavyset man, "I'll get you in to hear Mr. Moody. Here, take hold of my coat-tail."

So, Paul took hold of the short man's coat-tail. "Hold on now," said the man, "and don't let loose."

So he went all the way up the aisle and onto the great platform, holding onto the strange man's coat-tail. He was shown a seat in the second row.

When the chairman of the meeting said, "Mr. Moody will now preach," the man on whose coat-tail Rader had been hanging rose to preach.

Paul Rader had not known until then that he had been hanging onto the coat-tail of D. L. Moody, the world's most famous evangelist, founder of Moody Church and Moody Bible Institute.

Nor did Moody know that the boy who was hanging onto his coat-tail would be the man who, twenty-three years later, would be called as pastor of the Moody Church.

Paul Rader was reared at the top of the world and on the backbone of the North American continent—in Colorado and Wyoming. Extremely close to his father, whom he greatly admired, Rader was converted in Cheyenne at nine under his father's preaching. The elder Rader at the time was a missionary among the Indians.

Shortly afterward, a Methodist bishop who was staying in the Rader home asked Paul what he was going to do when he grew up.

"I want to be a preacher."

"Well," said the bishop, "then let us kneel here and ask God to make you a preacher." Both boy and bishop shed some tears in the emotional event, but Paul did not tell even his father of the incident until his sixteenth birthday, when he had already commenced to preach.

Athletic in stature, Rader learned to break broncos as a young teenager. By sixteen he had sung all over Colorado, traveling with his father. They called his dad "Cow-catcher Rader," because when a new town was built the missionary—and the saloon-keeper—would both be on the train's cow-catcher to be early arrivals. Often young Paul joined them.

At sixteen he told his dad he had been called to preach.

"Paul, why do you want to preach?" his dad asked.

"I have got to preach. I have been singing in the streets with the baby-organ in the city of Denver and helping old Jim Howell out in the mission every weekend."

"Have you got a call?"

"Yes, there is a rich man, one of your friends, a prominent lawyer, who has a camp of boys and wants me to come up and lead his boys to Christ."

The elder Rader sent his son, instead, to a remote town with a district of cowpunchers that he had wanted to reach for years. "I'll tell you how to get there. Tack a notice on the schoolhouse door, and there is an old lady who keeps a boarding house and the post-office, and there is a country store."

With less than $5 in his pocket, Paul Rader took the train to his assigned destination. He tacked his notice onto the schoolhouse and showed up the next day to find two present: the town's homely, wretched postmistress, for years despised by all in the area for her gossip and seamy life-style, and a deaf woman. The mission seemed useless, but Rader preached anyway.

The wretched old woman was converted and went throughout the countryside asking forgiveness of all those she had offended over the years. The deaf person heard words for the first time in ten years, rejoiced, and was also transformed.

Within hours, as word spread, the schoolhouse was packed with a crowd. No one knew how to sing a hymn, so Rader taught them one: "Just as I am, without one plea . . . ." He wrote the words on the chalkboard, pounded out the melody on the baby organ, and the crowd caught on.

> Just as I am without one plea,
> But that Thy Blood was shed for me.
> And that Thou bidd'st me come to Thee,
> O lamb of God, I come. I come.

"That's the way you will have to come, friends," Rader insisted.

When it came time for the sermon, he let the once wretched postmistress tell her story. Soon a big old blacksmith jumped up and said, "I want that." Others responded. Revival spread. Rader didn't know what to do. So he telegraphed his father for help. Eventually the elder Rader rolled into the train station with the crowd singing "Just as I am." Already seventy had been saved. Immediately father and son established a thriving church there.

Young Rader continued to preach. In his university years, under the influence of liberal theology, he drifted from his evangelical faith, though he still pursued the pastorate. But his ministry, he knew, was a sham. In New York City God called him back on course. Rader preached two years in Pittsburgh, then arranged evangelistic campaigns in Toledo, St. Paul, Chicago. In 1915, Moody Church called him to its pulpit.

The old Moody Church was not big enough to contain the crowds, even though Rader often addressed three audiences in one evening. The church looked for a new site. They found it in a large triangular lot at the corner of North Avenue and North Clark, at the southern end of Lincoln Park.

The church constructed a steel structure of tabernacle proportions, seating about 5,000 persons. The tabernacle was opened November 7, 1915. Night after night, week after week, and for months, Rader spoke each evening to vast multitudes. Thousands heard the gospel and responded. By 1917 the church, under Rader, had added 1,240 members. Associate pastor E. W. Woolley worked alongside. Songleader and soloist Arthur W. McKee became to Rader's ministry what Sankey was to Dwight Moody's.

During Rader years, the church acquired what became Cedar Lake Conference in Indiana. Formerly under the management of brewery interests, it was given to the Moody Church by the Monon Railway, to be used for religious purposes. During the summers, thousands poured to the site, also named "Rest-a-While," for Bible conferences, the annual church picnic, and other events, many taking the railroad to get there.

Some of Moody Church's senior citizens today still carry rich memories of the Paul Rader days. He left a deep impression on church poetess-songwriter Avis Christensen, who joined the church as a teenager on the same day that Paul Rader's wife and children became members. "He was a real 'go-getter,'" she recalled, "a dynamic speaker who used his whole body to preach. He gave long altar calls, walking up and down the aisles, personally inviting people to come forward." And, along with Avis Christensen, many did respond and later became leaders in Christian ministry.

During his years as pastor, Rader held thousands of meetings at the tabernacle with its wooden benches and dirt floors. Mrs. Christiansen remembered his taking a group of young people from the Christian Companionship Club to the University of Illinois in Urbana. "They had several meetings there and also did personal work. He was a great one to get people involved doing things."

Esther Filkin grew up at Moody Church during the days of Paul Rader. She vividly remembers one sermon he preached against liquor when she was quite young. She was eating a piece of licorice as he thundered, "I can smell the liquor on your breath!" Startled, and a bit scared, she asked her father, "Can he smell the licorice I'm eating?"

During Rader's ministry, a choir 200-strong, brass band, and orchestra participated in the services. Mrs. Filkin, as a child, played the piccolo in that orchestra. She was so small they had to set her up on the pulpit so she could be seen and then hold onto her feet to keep her from slipping off.

Ken Safstrom played in the brass band for a number of years as he was growing up. When the congregation moved from the tabernacle into the new church building, however, the brass band was discontinued. Evelyn Johnson also grew up during the days of Rader. When she was only four years old, she ran up on the platform during a service, telling Mr. Rader to "look at her new hairbow." An usher quickly retrieved her. (Evelyn Johnson's father was the chairman of building the new church in 1925 and was the one who handed over the keys from the architect to Pastor Philpott.)

The oldest living member of Moody Church today is Andy Wyzenbeek, age 95. The father of Esther Filkin, he joined the church in 1912, even before Rader had arrived. He was born again during a Billy Sunday meeting in Iowa, but the groundwork for his conversion had been laid when six profane Swedish mechanics with whom he worked at a factory in Ottumwa suddenly all became Christians. Wyzenbeek later distributed the story of these men and his own conversion in a tract entitled *Six Dirty Swedes*.

Peter Deyneka, Sr., founder of the Slavic Gospel Association that reaches into the countries of Eastern Europe, turned from atheism to a long and dynamic life of gospel evangelism under the ministry of Paul Rader and Moody Church.

The Russian immigrant, according to Deyneka's biography, "first heard of Moody Church on the streetcorners of Chicago when he was told he could hear eloquent English spoken by a public Speaker in a place called 'Moody Memorial Church' on Clark Street and North Avenue.

"Deyneka expected to find a small auditorium with a handful of old people. Instead he found four thousand people of all ages sitting on wooden benches in a huge tabernacle with sawdust sprinkled on the floor.

"'More Christians!' Peter murmured. He was tempted to leave, but the beauty of the music held him. Besides, it was Sunday and there was nothing better to do.

"As Paul Rader amplified his sermon, Peter felt smaller and smaller. He was convinced that someone had tipped off the preacher about the young Russian's sinful life.

"'You, there, you need to be born again!' Rader shouted time after time, pointing his long finger at the audience, always seeming to pick Peter out of the crowd. His heart raced. How could this man know so much about him—a total stranger?

"Peter detected another voice that evening, a conviction inside him, speaking unmistakably: *You are a lost sinner . . . Christ died for you . . . whosoever believes in Him will not perish.*"

Deyneka went forward at the invitation on the night of January 18, 1920, at age 22, turned his back forever upon his hard-drinking habits, and soon set his heart upon reaching Russia with the gospel.

Paul Rader's fame as a preacher of eloquence earned him respect from a broad cross-section of the public. The late news commentator Lowell Thomas, while teaching speech at Northwestern University, would send his students down to Moody Church to hear Paul Rader because, in the view of Thomas, "*There* is an orator."

In August 1921, Rader notified the church's executive committee that he had received a call from the New York Gospel Tabernacle, associated with the Christian and Missionary Alliance. During his years at Moody Church he had allowed himself to be named president of the Alliance, a move not cleared by the church. Some feared he might try to draw Moody Church into the Alliance, which would have been contrary to its historic nondenominational character. There was also concern that these extra duties had interfered with his Moody Church pastorate.

Meanwhile, the tabernacle, with its sawdust floors and hard wooden benches, had outlived the intent of its builders, who had originally conceived it as a temporary structure to accommodate a six-month evangelistic campaign. Surrounded by a rather unsightly fence of billboards, it was falling into disrepair.

But although the tabernacle may not have been a work of any architectural beauty, in it thousands of people, under the anointed ministry of Paul Rader, had found the Savior.

4

P. W. Philpott: The Building Years (1922-1929)

Dwight Moody, as a teenager in the hills of New England, chopped wood. The man Moody Church called to its pulpit in the early 1920s started his career as a blacksmith. Both men were reared by widowed mothers. To both God gave the gift of evangelism.

Long before he came to Moody Church, P. W. Philpott earned a reputation as one of Canada's foremost preachers. Thirty years earlier he had opened a gospel hall in Hamilton, Ontario—a faith venture for him and his wife and growing family, which eventually included thirteen children, eight sons and five daughters.

The work grew with the passing years. From a brick tabernacle seating 1,600 the church eventually had to utilize a theater seating 3,000 to accommodate Sunday evening services. Half a dozen new churches developed as off-shoots from his tabernacle in Toronto. He was in demand throughout America as a conference speaker.

Twice Philpott was urged to accept nomination to Canada's Parliament, with the understanding that if elected he would be made a member of the Cabinet. He turned down the tempting offers without hesitation.

Like D. L. Moody, Philpott was, in the main, a man of one book, the Bible—and the graduate of the school of life and sacrificial service. He was not self-made, but God-taught and trained through the Word and experience until thousands never tired of listening to him deliver God's message.

Philpott had long known and admired Moody Church. At the outset of his pastoral career, in fact, he had written to Moody Church for a copy of its constitution. Then he organized his own work along the same lines. But after a time, Philpott sensed a degree of failure. He attended a series of meetings held by D. L. Moody in Toronto. There he saw that the source of Moody's strength was the preaching of God's Word. From that time on a strong Bible ministry became his own supreme emphasis.

The wooden tabernacle in which Rader preached had been designed for only a six-month series of meetings. It was used for ten years. And for nearly three of those years, it accommodated evangelistic meetings six nights a week.

After Philpott's arrival, a visitor arose in a prayer meeting one night and said:

"I got in from Kentucky today. I wanted to see Mr. Moody's church. At the Institute, they sent me to Clark and North Avenue, but all I saw were billboards. At last I found the door and opened it and found this unsightly place." She waved her arms. "Surely you could build something better for such a great man as Mr. Moody."

All one Saturday night, Philpott prayed about the need. The next morning he told his congregation, "It is time to rise up and build."

> If ever a congregation needed a better "workshop," it is the Moody Church. The present building was erected for a six months' campaign. It has now served for over six years and is in a most wretched condition. The dirt floor, dingy walls and the uncomfortable seats have long since lost their attraction—the tabernacle has outlived its usefulness. It must be replaced, and for this purpose the church will need to have in sight $500,000 to start with. But the need is so real and so great that we are sure of Divine blessing upon the undertaking.

The church mobilized its forces for the task. The proposed memorial structure in tribute to Dwight L. Moody that eventually unfolded on the drawing boards seemed almost breathtaking, especially for a congregation that had lived for six years in a wooden structure with sawdust floors and surrounded by a fence of billboards.

The executive committee engaged as architects the firm of Fugard and Knapp, which had among its many credits the Allerton Hotel on Michigan Avenue. It hired as general contractor J. H. Johnson, an active Evangelical Free Church layman, who at that time had already built nearly thirty churches in Chicago and throughout the country.

The architects found their inspiration for Moody Memorial Church in northern Italy. They sought for a massive look—and a building of permanence—yet a style that would not contradict its theology or destroy its pocketbook. And so they drew heavily upon two church styles there that caught their eye.

In Italy's Lombard region they saw massive Romanesque churches some

900 years old that had made good use of brick and terra cotta. These churches, perhaps more than anything else, prompted the architects to think brick rather than stone. (Cut stone would be costly, as would exterior stone trimming, builders pointed out.) And interior brick walls would never have to be repainted.

The architects even suggested that the form of worship in these Romanesque churches at that earlier time of history may have been closer to New Testament theology than one might at first think. They noted, for instance, the wide column spacing in some of these structures. That suggested that the churches then may have held preaching more central than ritual.

But it was the early Christian church of St. Sophia that gave builders, in part, the architectural style. For they had to create a structure that would accommodate large capacity, yet give everyone clear view of the pulpit. A theatre-style could have accomplished this, but that would have been unarchitectural. A cathedral would have housed the congregation, but a cathedral is designed for a ritualistic service, which is contrary to the tenets of Moody Church.

The St. Sophia church could seat a vast multitude in an unimpeded auditorium. And so St. Sophia gave Moody Church its large sanctuary, supporting pillars, and half dome at the Clark Street end. Oriental workmen, however, had built St. Sophia lavish and rich in character. The architects adapted to give Moody Church simplicity. Such a blend makes Moody Church architecturally unique among the churches of America.

The *Moody Church News*, April 1925, offered other interesting details:

> There will be thirty-six large windows in the auditorium, but none of them will be used for ventilating, hence there will be no drafts to jeopardize the health of either preacher or hearers. Through the ventilating system installed by the engineers the entire air content of the auditorium during services will be changed every six minutes.
>
> The structure is fully equipped for the installation of a radio broadcasting station if required; and facilities are provided also for loud speaker equipment. One section of seats in the auditorium will be equipped with head phones [for the hard of hearing].
>
> The Church proper is an enormous room. The ceiling will be as high as a six-story building, but the room is so long and so wide that the height will not be felt. The main floor will be a grand sweep of 2,270 seats, curved so the view will be satisfactory from any seat. The balcony contains 1,470 seats....
>
> The Moody Memorial Church is ideally situated, facing Lincoln Park on the one side and LaSalle Avenue on the other. Transportation is of the best. Clark street carries the greatest volume of north-and-south street car traffic, North Avenue is convenient for the east-and-west, while LaSalle Avenue is on our boulevard system.

The people prayed and pledged. There were few wealthy people among them, but with great love for God and deep devotion to His cause, they went forward. The first step was the sale of the North Avenue frontage for $300,000.

At last Moody Church broke ground for its new edifice. By March 1925, the old Moody Tabernacle was down. The congregation held its last service there on Sunday, March 15. It then moved back into its old building at Chicago and LaSalle, which had been purchased by Moody Bible Institute, until construction could be completed. The old Moody Church would also soon be razed.

The church issued bonds to raise cash as the work progressed. It experienced a setback when excavation for the foundation revealed quicksand. Extra thousands of dollars were needed to make a solid foundation for the large building. During the Depression days, when most bonds were being discounted, Moody Church bonds were being redeemed at 100 percent face value. Every pledge to the church was met—except in the case of an investor's total loss or death.

When word came that the insurance company holding the mortgage had to raise interest rates, Philpott put the need before the people. In one day members took over the remaining debt themselves.

The new church would need thousands of chairs. Members met that need by purchasing them one, two, or three at a time, mostly in memorials to loved ones.

On Sunday morning, November 8, 1925, the new home of the Moody Memorial Church was dedicated. It sat on ground valued at $500,000, with buildings and equipment costing nearly $1,000,000. Every one of its 4,040 seats was filled, and hundreds stood through the whole service in the ambulatory surrounding the cantilever balcony. Golden sunlight flooded the auditorium, and, coming through amber-tinted windows, it lost none of its glory and retained none of its glare. It touched the audience and the speakers with what seemed to many a radiance almost divine.

In his dedicatory sermon that morning, which focused on the life of D. L. Moody and his world wide impact, Philpott told his people that the new building was to stand "as a memorial to one of Chicago's greatest citizens."

Even Chicago newspapers acknowledged that perhaps no other individual of early Chicago had made the city so well known—in a favorable way—as Dwight L. Moody. In far-away India, for example, the *Bombay Gazette,* in an article on Chicago's problems and attributes, called Dwight L. Moody "the patron saint of Chicago."

Ironically, less than two years later, the Valentine Day Massacre and the escapades of Al Capone would give Chicago a somewhat different reputation that continues to haunt the city to this day.

Philpott said Chicago was the logical place for Moody's monument, for it was "here that he began his ministry and here he learned the secret of reaching men." It was also, he said, "the first of all institutions founded by him.

> This building shall ever stand as a testimony to the power of the gospel of God's grace.... Our church now has a membership of 3,436 and 88 of our members are missionaries in foreign lands.... We ask the question , "What mean these stones?" They mean that there is a great Protestant church in the city of Chicago where rich and poor alike are ever welcome and where in spirit and in truth they can worship the God who is the maker of us all.
>
> They mean also that this church is to be a base from which heralds of the cross will be sent forth in greater numbers to the ends of the earth to tell the story of redeeming grace.

The next day Philpott accepted an honorary doctorate from Wheaton College and became Dr. Philpott. Special events followed every night for nearly two weeks. Then on November 22, Reuben A. Torrey arrived for an evangelistic campaign at Moody Church. A quarter century earlier he had left the pastorate of Moody Church— and then also the presidency of Moody Bible Institute—to conduct crusades worldwide: in Australia, New Zealand, Japan, India, and other lands. With a new building it was now time to remind the church, perhaps, that a monument of bricks, in itself, would not be enough. The gospel must go forth in spiritual power.

Though the assault of theological liberalism continued to erode the Protestant church at large, Moody Church and many like it across the country stood firm.

On Sunday, December 20, evangelist Billy Sunday took the pulpit:

> "There is no name like Jesus," the evangelist said. "It is more imperial than Caesar's. It is more conquering than Charlemagne's. It is more eloquent than Cicero's. It is more inspiring than George Washington's. The name Jesus weeps with pathos. It groans with all pain. It breathes perfume. Who like Jesus can mend a broken heart? Who but Jesus can bring the prodigal back to the Father's arms and the Father's heart? Oh, friends, Jesus is all the world to me!"

In a defense of the virgin birth, Philpott declared:

> I place no limitations on what God Almighty can do. I believe the Bible literally and verbally. I would not worship a God that could not move in a realm beyond my comprehension and do things that I cannot do.
>
> Atheists and Modernists sometimes make so much noise in declaring their

beliefs, that one is inclined to suppose that there is left only a very small minority which believes in the whole Bible.

But Philpott took heart in a religious census taken by American newspapers, among them the *Chicago Daily News*. The results were printed on the front page of the *Moody Church News:*

1. Do you believe in God? Yes, 89 percent; no, 11 percent.
2. Do you believe in immortality? Yes, 85 percent; no, 15 percent.
3. Do you believe that Jesus was divine as no other man was divine? Yes, 77 percent; no, 23 percent.
4. Do you regard the Bible as inspired in a sense that no other literature could be said to be inspired? Yes, 80 percent; no, 20 percent.
5. Are you an active member of any church? Yes, 70 percent; no, 30 percent.
6. Were you brought up in a religious home? Yes, 88 percent; no, 12 percent.
7. Do you think that religion in some form is a necessary element of life for the individual and the community? Yes, 90 percent; no, 10 percent.

Once into its new building, the Moody Church Sunday school, under Philpott's counsel, changed its meeting time from afternoon to morning before church services. The church took its cue from other prominent evangelical churches in America that had made the move—including congregations in Ft. Worth, Minneapolis, and New York City, who saw Sunday school attendance rise dramatically with the change. It was a bold stroke at the time, though many today are surprised to learn that the Sunday morning time slot was not always traditional.

The decision came not without initial objections. Would it not be difficult for many families living at a distance from the church, some asked, to get their children ready in time? Others wondered if young people who no longer could attend afternoon Sunday school might get into more mischief. And would not the church lose those who attended their own church Sunday schools in the morning and Moody Church's Sunday school in the afternoon?

But with the move growth resulted, and the change united the church and Sunday school into a more cohesive unit.

The renowned English Bible expositor G. Campbell Morgan came to Moody Church in 1927 and preached for seven consecutive Sunday mornings. He had first visited the United States in 1896, coming as far west as "Moody's church in Chicago."

Dr. Morgan praised the people for their new edifice but apparently sensed that it could hamper Philpott's ministry if the church allowed it to do so. "I charge you officers of this church," he told the congregation, "to lift this burden off the shoulders of this man. He should be absolutely free from any care about finances."

The Moody Church missions program continued to grow through the 1920s, and the *Moody Church News* continued to give its readers monthly field reports. The 1926 missions conference generated $43,000 in cash and pledges. But the church was shocked when it received news that one of its missionaries, Morris Slichter, and his three-year-old daughter, Ruth Irene, had been martyred by Chinese bandits near Yunnanfu.

Many other Moody-supported missionaries also served in China, and a lengthy article in May 1928, entitled "The Dawn of China's New Day," reported that church membership in China had doubled amid persecution.

In June of that same year the church ordained Ralph T. Davis, whose record of six years with the Africa Inland Mission had already proved exceptional. Later Davis would become director of the entire mission and see it grow to become one of the world's largest.

Another item in the *Moody Church News* reports the return of Guy Playfair to his work in Nigeria. Almost two decades later, in 1944, he would become general director of the Sudan Interior Mission upon the death of its founder and head, R. V. Bingham. Playfair had gone to Africa under SIM in 1910, when it had only seventeen missionaries. It later expanded into an organization with more than one thousand missionaries, one of the largest faith missions in the world.

World-famed evangelist Gipsy Smith came to Moody Church for a campaign in December 1927. While men like Gipsy Smith, Billy Sunday, and G. Campbell Morgan preached campaigns in Moody Church during the twenties, Philpott conducted during this same decade some impressive campaigns of his own. In October 1927, at the request of Christian businessmen in the Twin Cities, Philpott led a city-wide evangelistic campaign. Thousands crowded into the City Auditorium each night, and the response seemed to verge on revival.

Early in 1928 Philpott led another city-wide campaign, this time in Tacoma, Washington. Members of Moody Church covenanted to pray that a heaven-sent revival might come to that city. God seemed to move in a special way. Under the supervision of Philpott's Moody Church associate Arthur W. McKee, in charge of music for the meetings, a temporary tabernacle seating 6,300 was erected in exactly eighteen hours!

The call to evangelism proved a strong one. In the spring of 1929, only months before the stock market crash, Philpott announced his resignation, effective June 30, to do evangelistic and Bible conference work. During Philpott's seven years the church had built a million-dollar edifice, and regular attendance was larger than at any other time in the church's history. "You have been a most delightful people to serve," he reassured all.

5

Harry Ironside: The Teaching Years (1930-1948)

Harry Ironside was never formally ordained, nor had he any previous pastoral experience when, in 1930, he stepped into the pulpit of Moody Church.

Yet during his eighteen years as pastor there, he became the archbishop of American fundamentalism and a by-word in evangelical circles everywhere. Ironside was said to have "access to more pulpits than any other man in the country." He filled Moody Memorial Church's vast auditorium for nearly two decades, and in his first fourteen years he saw only two Sundays in which there was not at least one public profession of Christ.

Ironside's formal education did not go beyond grammar school. Yet his breadth of knowledge made him at home with scholars in many fields, whether Old Testament archaeology or Chinese literature.

His life was the favorite "log cabin to White House" story of a poor boy who made good.

At the hour of Ironside's birth, the attending physician pronounced him dead and laid him aside to attend to his mother. But forty minutes later the startled nurse detected signs of pulse and plunged him into a hot bath, from which he emerged on October 14, 1876, alive and healthy.

Ironside's father had been a godly preacher in Toronto, then Los Angeles, though he died when Harry was only two. When Dwight L. Moody came to Los Angeles, Ironside found Hazzard's Pavilion packed to the door. The young towhead pushed his way into the balcony to hear the famous preacher but found no seat. Noticing that the roof was supported by girders made of 4" × 12" planks spiked together like a trough, young Ironside skinned up the slanting trough to a point high over the crowd, looking down on the platform. The forceful manner and earnestness of the bearded evangelist and the singing that night moved the boy's heart. "Lord, help me someday," he prayed, "to preach to crowds like these and to lead souls to Christ."

By the time he was ten, he had read the Bible through ten times. When he found no Sunday school in his neighborhood, he set out to start one. In a homemade burlap tent, precocious Harry taught the Bible to a class of sixty, mostly children, but including some adults.

Yet it was not until age fourteen that he came under deep conviction of sin at a party and ran home to fall on his knees beside his bed and accept Christ as his Savior, finding in Romans 3 and John 3 the peace he had been seeking.

Ironside immediately began to preach everywhere—in missions, in churches, on the street. He soon became known as the "Boy Preacher of Los Angeles," and at age eighteen he had risen to the rank of captain in the Salvation Army. Later he identified with the Plymouth Brethren movement. At twenty-three he married the daughter of a Presbyterian minister, and the couple lived for years on a bare existence, while Ironside continued to preach—in all kinds of settings and circumstances.

Before a crowd of several hundred on a street corner in San Francisco one evening, he was challenged by a prominent atheist to a debate on Christianity versus atheism. Ironside agreed, on one condition. The atheist would have to present at least 2 bona fide witnesses who had been saved from lives of disgrace and degradation by their belief, while he would provide no fewer than 100 who had been saved from the same state by the gospel of Christ.

Hurriedly the atheist declined the terms and left, to the delight of the crowd.

Ironside soon found himself preaching to crowds across the country. For ten years he also spent considerable time preaching among the Southwest Indians. More than one male child of Navajo or Mohave origin was named after him, and in later years, when he became pastor of Moody Church, Indians could often be seen in the congregation.

A voracious reader, Ironside devoured two to three books of substance a day and was said to have almost total recall of anything he had ever read.

When P. W. Philpott resigned in 1929, the church fathers looked seven months for his successor. Finally the church called Harry Ironside, by then fifty-three. It took him ten months to say yes, for he had never pastored a church before, and, for that matter, the idea of "pastor" was contrary to all settled practice of the Plymouth Brethren. Upon Ironside's acceptance, former pastor Philpott wrote, "Ironside under God will accomplish great things."

Upon his arrival at Moody Church, Ironside reminded the people that he had never been a candidate for the position. "It is a strange thing to get elected," he said, "when you never ran. But I accept the call as from God."

When he entered the pulpit his first Sunday morning, he faced a full congregation. Membership at that time stood at about 3,750. But the church also faced a building debt of $375,000, no small figure in those days—and in the midst of the Depression. The church originally was to have cost $800,000, but the final price tag climbed to over $1 million when the city decided to widen La Salle Street. This widening made it necessary to remove eighteen feet from the west front of the building as originally planned. These changes ordered by the city together with the necessary additional equipment for the entire building cost the church $239,000 in excess of what it had originally anticipated.

Also, the original five-year pledge program to cover the construction did not include interest on the gold bonds that the church had issued. Much of that—specifically $53,000—had to be met out of the building fund. And unpaid pledges during those years of economic stress had amounted to $83,000.

Yet in 1943 the church burned its mortgage. Under Ironside it had retired its indebtedness at the rate of $26,000 a year.

In preaching, Ironside drew upon a broad base of knowledge. When he delivered a sermon in 1932, for example, on the topic "Has the Sino-Japanese War Prophetic Significance?" ("Not much," he concluded, for most prophecy, geographically, revolves around Israel), he could offer his congregation evidence that the Chinese once knew something of biblical revelation. "Bible truth is manifested in the Chinese language," he observed, citing such Chinese characters as those for "lust" (a woman standing between two trees), "ark" (a boat and the character for *eight*) and other evidence. "The Chinese," he insisted, "lost the faith that once they had."

Some of the visitors to Chicago's 1933 World's Fair, or "Century of Progress," found their way to Moody Church. It was the heart of the Depression, of course, and the "Century of Progress" seemed to be whistling in the dark. The gospel offered a hope and prosperity that went beyond mere materialism. The church distributed to fairgoers 50,000 copies of R. A. Laidlaw's booklet *The Reason Why* and had some activity at the church every night of the fair for five months. Audiences at Moody Church during this period totaled 300,000.

Ironside made clear when he accepted the call to Moody Church that he wanted freedom to travel about the country during the week on the Bible conference circuit. He was out of the city for about forty weeks of each year. Leaving his suite in the Hotel Plaza across the street from the church on Monday, he would travel anywhere within a radius of 1,000 miles to hold meetings and return on Saturday afternoons to prepare his sermon for the next day and write lesson studies for the *Sunday School Times.*

With no outlines or notes, he preached extempore from a passage of Scripture, rarely on a topic. His preaching style may have seemed somewhat unspectacular, but he could expound the Scriptures masterfully for the common man and convey their practical value. On Sundays when Ironside was not in the pulpit, attendance fell, no matter how esteemed or prominent his replacement.

Some of today's Moody Church seniors remember him well. "In the pulpit," says Evelyn Johnson, "he just opened his Bible [bought new each year from the dime store] and talked, using no notes." George Cady remembers him as one who preached as though he were "just talking to you as a friend." He always had time for people, time to talk with them and find out what was on their hearts.

Nearly everything Ironside ever preached appeared in print, often transcribed from radio broadcasts of the church's Sunday morning services. His sermons filled scores of books—among them devotional commentaries hailed by some as the outstanding commentaries of the century. Many of his books were published by his own Western Book & Tract Company, which he financed and organized in 1914 in Oakland, California. Because of his prolific publishing, Ironside was known to many as an author, not a preacher.

Ironside made several trips abroad, and his acclaim in Great Britain was as wide as in the United States. He served on the boards of innumerable Christian organizations, lending his name to groups ranging from Bob Jones College (now University) to the National Association of Evangelicals.

Ironside liked nothing better than to sit down at a table, tuck a napkin high on his capacious bay, and, eyes twinkling, launch into a series of side-splitting stories and anecdotes about men he had met around the world. His excellent sense of humor included a wealth of Scottish dialect tales, but he governed his humor in the pulpit. He had one hobby—stamp collecting—and owned an almost professional collection of between 25,000 and 30,000 stamps.

Noted evangelist Gipsy Smith, who had conducted a campaign in Moody Church in 1927, returned again in 1933. An aggregate attendance of some 8,000 greeted him on the opening Sunday. Throughout his long career Gipsy Smith had spoken in almost every English-speaking country in the world and had appeared at Buckingham Palace ten times. He radiated a magnificent love for God and man that everyone seemed to sense. Years later many who heard him looked back on the event as a never-to-be-forgotten experience.

The next year Billy Sunday, professional ballplayer turned evangelist (Sunday had played for the old Chicago White Stockings), came to Moody church in the waning months of his life. Seven thousand crowded the premises to hear him. One year later, Moody Memorial Church was the site of his funeral. More than three thousand people filed past his casket. It was said that during Sunday's quarter century of evangelism, some one million people responded to the gospel. At the funeral Moody Church assistant pastor Homer A. Rodeheaver, who was for twenty years Sunday's close associate, asked all those who had been saved through Sunday's ministry to stand as a tribute to him. Many arose. It was a lengthy but memorable service. Many paid tribute from the platform, including Ironside, Moody Bible Institute's Will Houghton; Homer Rodeheaver; John Timothy Stone, pastor emeritus of Chicago's Fourth Presbyterian Church (Sunday had been a longtime member of the Chicago Presbytery); and Walter Taylor, super-intendent of the Pacific Garden Mission, where Sunday had been saved and which he later heavily funded with the offerings from his final Chicago campaign.

Although not one to major on politics, Ironside—and the church—pro-tested in 1933 President Franklin D. Roosevelt's overtures to the govern-ment of the Soviet Republic. The congregation drafted a resolution against such actions and sent it to the White House. "How any professed Christian country can expect the blessing of God to rest upon such an alliance," declared Ironside, "we cannot understand."

Some Moody Church highlights of the latter 1930s and early 1940s were:

1936: The Moody Italian Mission, under A. F. Scorza, relocated to the southwest corner of Elm and LaSalle. That same year Ironside registered nearly 70,000 miles on his trips at home and abroad—long before the jet age.

1937: Moody Church joined with Moody Bible Institute to celebrate the D. L. Moody Centenary. More than 2,300 churches in the United States and twenty nine foreign lands observed the evangelist's 100th birthday.

1938: On a Sunday morning in January, Charles E. Fuller's "Old Fash-ioned Revival Hour" was aired live coast to coast from Moody Church—to an estimated 5 million listeners. More than 17,000 people attended the several services and special events at the church on Easter Sunday that year.

1939: The old Moody Church on the corner of Chicago and LaSalle, which had also long doubled as Moody Bible Institute's auditorium, was razed to make room for Houghton Hall, MBI's ten-story women's dormi-tory. Special tickets to the farewell service were issued to those who had been saved in the historic building.

1940: War clouds gathered in Europe. Mr. and Mrs. J. S. Ferguson, Moody Church supported missionaries to Africa, narrowly escaped death when a German mine blew out the bottom of their ship enroute back to the field from furlough. The two lost all their possessions.

1941: The church celebrated Ironside's fifty years in the ministry.

Gipsy Smith, at age eighty, returned for a fifteen-day campaign. His first appearance in Chicago occurred in 1893, when Dwight L. Moody conducted international revival services at the Columbian Exposition. The *Chicago Daily News* reported that Gipsy Smith had "addressed more people perhaps than any living preacher."

John S. Ironside, former purser on the dollar Steamship Lines and son of the pastor, joined the Moody Church staff as assistant pastor.

Several more Moody Church missionaries escaped harm when the *SS Zam Zam* was torpedoed by the Nazis off the coast of Africa. The Japanese attacked Pearl Harbor, and Moody Church found it increasingly difficult to keep in touch with many of its missionaries. The church called for prayer, particularly for those "exposed to great danger."

1942: Gipsy Smith returned to Moody Church for a two-week citywide campaign. The church had booked Chicago's Coliseum but had to move the event back to the church when the War Department took over the building. He told 300 pastors of the Chicago Ministerial Association, "I have found in all these years that people want religion undiluted and they will pack the churches where the gospel of Christ is proclaimed."

1943: With World War II in midstream, the church listed 181 servicemen on its honor roll, with one gold star in memory of Maynard William Tollberg. One day, off Guadalcanal, a Japanese torpedo hit Tollberg's ship, and a shattering explosion released high pressure steam, which killed everybody in the engine room but Tollberg. Severely scalded, partly blinded, he groped over the bodies of dead comrades, and with his fast-ebbing strength, closed an oil valve, saving the lives of other trapped shipmates before he himself died. For extraordinary heroism, the Navy Cross was awarded posthumously. But even more precious was this letter from a shipmate: "Even since his death there have been some who have accepted Christ because of his testimony. He being dead yet speaketh." Later, the Navy further honored him by launching the USS *Tollberg*.

Before the war ended, the church had to add several other gold stars.

The church burned its mortgage on the final day of 1943. In 1946 Howard Hermansen rejoined Moody Church as associate pastor. The church received word that beloved Gipsy Smith had been called home. Meanwhile, the church hosted the first annual convention of the National Sunday School Association. The next year Bob Murfin, a household name to today's listeners of radio WMBI, was hired as the church's youth director. Upon arrival in Chicago, someone saw the Indiana farmboy climb out of a taxi at Moody Bible Institute, kick his toe quizzically against the curb, and exclaim, "Well, it's no wonder they built these big buildings here. The ground is too hard to plant corn anyway!"

On May 30, 1948, Ironside announced his resignation after eighteen years, citing his wife's health as a major factor. The two had already purchased a little home at Winona Lake, Indiana. But even before the resignation could be acted upon the Lord called Mrs. Ironside home, four months after their golden wedding anniversary.

Ironside still considered his decision non-negotiable. He continued his ministry on the Bible conference circuit that he loved so well. Cataract operations in September 1950 restored his failing sight. The following January he visited New Zealand for a preaching mission. Before the engagement was over, he suffered a fatal heart attack on January 15, 1951.

Harry Ironside used to say that he did not want an elaborate marker—just a simple one reading:

> HARRY A. IRONSIDE
> Sinner saved by grace
> Moved out until renovated
> and repaired

6

Franklin Logsdon: The Transition Years (1951-1952)

Two years after the resignation of Harry Ironside, Moody Church called to its pulpit S. Franklin Logsdon, pastor of the Central Baptist Church of London, Ontario. Highly respected as a Bible expositor, Logsdon, then forty-four, had served pastorates in Maryland and Pennsylvania. An American citizen, he was born in the Cumberland mountains of western Maryland.

On the evening of his installation, as the church warmly welcomed its new pastor, a cablegram arrived from Cambridge, New Zealand. Harry Ironside, it announced, had died in his sleep while on a Bible teaching tour in that land. The happiness of the evening suddenly turned to sadness.

Thankful for what Ironside had meant to Moody Church, however, its people looked to the future. One month later, on the opening night of Moody Bible Institute's Founder's Week, 10,000 people packed out two services to hear evangelist Billy Graham. "There is a desperate need of revival," said Graham. "The world is on the brink of chaos, and our nation is done for unless it has a revival." But on the flip side of the coin, Graham noted that "last year more people attended the churches of the nation than any year in the history of America."

Unlike Ironside, who for nearly two decades spent most of the workweek away from Moody Church, Logsdon took a more hands-on approach to day-by-day church affairs. This required an adjustment for both pastor and board.

In the fall of that same year, Wheaton College bestowed upon Logsdon an honorary doctorate, the church hosted another successful Greater Chi-

cago Sunday School Convention, with Henrietta Mears and Bob Jones, Jr.,
both keynoters, and the *Moody Church News* carried an interesting letter
from Matthew B. Ridgway, General, United States Army, and head of the
Supreme Command of the Allied Powers in Japan. It was written in response to the concern of mission leaders over the dismissal of General
Douglas MacArthur.

"Please express to the members of your organization [The Evangelical
Alliance Mission] my sincere appreciation for the special greeting which
you extended to me in your letter. I am fully conscious of the great work
which your missionaries are carrying on in Japan, and you may be assured
that I shall always extend the utmost cooperation to the carrying on of
their missionary efforts. With every good wish, sincerely [signed] M. B.
Ridgway."

The statement was interpreted as a continued favorable attitude enjoyed
by missionaries under the leadership of General MacArthur. Early in 1950
TEAM's board chairman, T. J. Bach, had had an interview with MacArthur,
who requested: "Please send ten missionaries for every one you have here
now."

Moody Church had long supported some of those missionaries.

In July 1952, Logsdon submitted his resignation to accept the pastorate
of the Immanuel Church of Holland, Michigan. Although he esteemed his
short tenure an honor, Logsdon concluded that "my heart dictates my
move."

Dr. Logsdon was graciously received by the church, but his philosophy
of leadership differed from that of the Executive Committee. Since Ironside
had not been directly involved in the administration of the church, the
board thought that Dr. Logsdon should follow that example.

Logsdon today still speaks warmly of the church leadership, however.
"They were good men who loved the Lord and desired to be led by Him,"
he recalls. "But I wanted to be more directly involved in the direction of the
church, so I thought it best to resign to avoid possible conflict."

7

Alan Redpath: The Keswick Years (1953-1962)

Alan Redpath had been an accountant with one of England's largest commercial firms before God called him from his promising business career into the ministry.

A natural athlete and rugby player, he was converted in an English tavern by a business colleague.

Redpath tells the story:

> I had been around that man's life for some three years before it happened. I got angry with him; I did everything I could to discourage him, to knock Christianity out of him, to prove to him that his religion was wrong. He annoyed me intensely, simply because he was living a standard of life that I was not prepared to live.

The man's Spirit-filled witness finally turned Redpath around, and a dramatic change of life-style followed.

Redpath came to Moody Church in 1953 from the pastorate of the Duke Street Baptist Church of London, which he had transformed from an obscure chapel into one of the most thriving Free Churches in the land. When Sunday evening crowds outgrew the building, he rented a large theater for evangelistic services.

Of his first Christmas away from England Redpath wrote, "To be quite honest, we have missed the Old Country. But you have all been so wonderful to us...."

The heat of Chicago surfaced frequently in Redpath's diary notes, which appeared each month in the *Moody Church News* throughout his years as pastor. "Very hot in church today. Temperature at about ninety degrees and humidity ninety-three per cent. Didn't find preaching easy on a day like this, but trust the Lord blessed in it all. Hallelujah anyway."

"The thunderstorms we have around here," he wrote in his notes in June 1954, are certainly outstanding. The one we had last night is the nearest I can remember to a London air-raid!"

Other touches of England surfaced. One hundred young people from Christianaires and Homebuilders squeezed into the parsonage one evening early in his tenure for what was labeled the church's first "squash." In England the term meant a popular handball sport. At Moody Church it meant a crowded social event designed to reach out to new folk with the gospel.

Redpath and the church looked outward and saw spiritual need. The public at large mostly ignored the claims of Jesus Christ upon their lives. Yet this interesting item appeared in the *Moody Church News*, July 1954:

> The Chicago city council recently passed a resolution calling on Congress to add the words "under God" to the pledge of allegiance. The bill to change the pledge was submitted to Congress by Senator Ferguson of Michigan." [A short time later, under the Eisenhower administration, the U.S. Congress altered the wording to give America the now familiar phrase "One nation under God . . . ."]

But such words can be little more than symbolic, and Redpath saw the need of a deeper spiritual work in the lives of God's people, Moody Church no exception. So in 1954 he assembled the church's first Mid-America Keswick Convention, with its emphasis on personal revival and holy living. The Keswick movement had its origin in England, and its message was obviously a major part of Redpath's heartbeat.

"It must never be imagined," said Redpath, "that Keswick teaching, which, of course, is nothing other than New Testament holiness of life put into practice, is merely inward and introspective." He spoke, instead, of lives "submitted to the Sovereignty of the Lord in every detail."

> Fundamentalism today has been guilty, in my humble judgement, of presenting the message of forgiveness of sins through the Atonement of our Lord Jesus Christ without at the same time, in many cases, presenting the message of deliverance from the principles of sin through the Cross, and by the power of the indwelling Spirit. This is not merely half a Gospel; it is no Gospel at all.

"This double message of full salvation is the main inward thrust of any church," insisted Redpath, "if her testimony is to be vital. Toplady knew full well what he was saying when he wrote:

> 'Let the water and the blood,
> From Thy riven side which flowed,
> Be of sin the *double* cure,
> Cleanse me from its guilt and power.'"

By 1958, the fifth annual Mid-America Keswick Convention drew registrants from thirty-two different states and more than forty different denominations. At one meeting during the week, eighty-seven people responded to the challenge for the mission field.

Redpath had little patience for the kind of theology that over-dispensationalized the Bible:

"I believe that one of Satan's greatest triumphs has been to persuade evangelical Christians that the Sermon on the Mount is not for this age of grace. Somehow it speaks to my soul with tremendous conviction."

Despite a certain English reserve, Redpath was not afraid at times to bare his heart: "Two good congregations today," reads a Sunday entry in his diary in the *Moody Church News*. "I believe the Lord is continuing to speak to hearts. How much I need Him constantly to speak to me. How often my prayer is:

> 'Lord, speak to me, that I may speak
> In living echoes of Thy tone.'"

Words quoted from a hymn often prefaced his prayers from the platform:

> "Speak, Lord in the stillness, as we wait on Thee;
> Hushed, our souls to listen in expectancy."

But his warmth and humor, along with admission of his own mistakes, also came through, as in this entry dated Monday, March 14, 1955:

> Returned today after a very blessed few days at the Bible Conference in Atlanta.... What a lovely place Atlanta is—just a bit too hot for my liking, however.
> I got to the railway station, sat down in the train, which never departed. I discovered about an hour later that there was a strike on, and that I was the only passenger on the train, which didn't even have an engine attached to it. Did I feel stupid.

When on one occasion a mother introduced her little girl to the new pastor, the child looked up into his face and remarked in surprise, "Oh, I thought you were an Indian!" The name *Redpath* had misled her.

Moody Church has long accommodated many of the city's major evangelical events, and in the Redpath era that tradition continued. In 1954 it hosted the Greater Chicago Sunday School convention and in 1956 an even larger event; the National Sunday School Association convention itself.

The church has long known how to handle large gatherings, and over the years its well-trained "Usher Band" has developed crowd control into almost a science. It is a task that can demand professional skills. "Have you ever watched an usher start from the back of a church with a would-be worshiper following him," Redpath once observed, "only to discover that by the time the usher had reached the seat he had in mind, he had long been walking down the aisle alone?"

Some ushers have served for decades, as have some of the deacons and elders on the church's executive committee, which traditionally numbers in excess of sixty. In 1954 George B. Meeker, still young at heart, marked fifty years from the day he was first elected to the Moody Church Executive Committee.

The Redpath family sailed for England on the Queen Mary in late May 1957. A week later found him in Carlisle, a city near the Scottish border and adjoining the ancient Hadrian Wall, the boundary of the Roman Empire.

"I had an evangelistic campaign here ten years ago," he wrote in his diary, "and it has been wonderful tonight to meet some of the converts. One of them now in the ministry in this city ... another on the mission field in Africa. Praise the Lord for fruit that has remained. This, after all, surely is what ultimately matters."

Redpath admired the initiative of Christians who found ways to take the gospel to the people where they were, even if by unorthodox method:

Sunday, August 28, 1955: "Preached today at Lancaster, Pennsylvania, at a Drive-in Church. Some 700 people present in about 300 cars. A great opportunity, but a problem exists in making contact with people whom you never see because they remain in their cars and drive away at the end of the service. Praise the Lord, however, for the initiative of His people."

In April 1957, the church received word that P. W. Philpott had been called home to be with the Lord. Under his ministry today's great edifice had been built. Philpott had left the pulpit of Moody Church in 1929 to serve at the Church of the Open Door in Los Angeles, then spent twelve years as associate to Oswald J. Smith of the Peoples Church, Toronto.

Some further entries from "Pastor's Diary":

October 10, 1957: Redpath first mentions the possibility of a Billy Graham campaign in Chicago. "While I do not think a Billy Graham Campaign could ever be the final answer to the need of the city," he writes, "it would certainly be a great contibution towards it and one which we at Moody Church would greatly welcome."

Sunday, July 13, 1958. "Hallelujah! This has been a day of great victory. At the close of the morning service the Lord brought more than a hundred people to publicly confess their powerlessness and their need of Christ as Lord. The greatest response I have seen in almost five years."

From the outset of his ministry at Moody Church, Redpath stressed neighborhood visitation. "For a metropolitan church to become no more than a preaching station in which large numbers of people assemble to listen to a preacher and to be spectators of a program, rather than to be personally committed to the task of evangelism, is to spell the doom of such a fellowship and to write "Ichabod" over the door.

That concern deepened as, year by year, Moody Church families migrated out of the city to the suburbs, and the neighborhood around the church took on an ever more cosmopolitan look.

"The immediate neighborhood surrounding the church is nothing less than an international mission field," Redpath declared.

> Eastward as far as Lake Michigan, a distance of about half a mile, but covering an area of some three miles in length, exists a population diverse in the extreme. Many are wealthy people living by the lakeshore; others mostly business people. North, south, and westward it is entirely different. Here Puerto Ricans and other nationalities have moved into the area by the thousands, many of them with very little knowledge of the English language.
>
> Hundreds of others had moved up from the Southern states to seek better employment and a higher standard of life. They live, for the most part, in poor tenement buildings and in squalid surroundings.

In addition to this mix, Moody Bible Institute lay within a mile to the south on LaSalle. Many of its more than one thousand students made Moody Church their home church.

"Within two miles of this church," observed Redpath, "are indeed all sorts and conditions of men."

Redpath attempted to shift the emphasis of evangelistic preaching from Sunday services in church to a sense of greater personal responsibility in the home. The membership of the church was divided into twenty-five groups, each one under the supervision of a deacon or an elder. Each group was asked to meet monthly for prayer and fellowship.

These meetings were built in part around conversational Bible study and prayer. It was an attempt to unite an increasingly scattered membership into little cells of Christian fellowship where there could be a sense of unity and mutual concern for others.

To accommodate the Spanish-speaking people, the church initiated a

Sunday school class conducted in Spanish by missionaries on furlough from Spanish-speaking countries.

Redpath cited the high turnover in the enrollment of the Sunday school because of the transient factor. "Because of this turnover we cannot build up the membership of Moody Church through our Sunday school, but then that is not our primary task. It seems to me that we are not called upon to build *up* anything, but rather to build the church *out*."

Many in the church worried about the steady drift of families to the suburbs. Redpath reminded them, "We cannot expect anything else in a metropolitan area of this kind. Nevertheless, unless we can replace them with other families, the church just cannot maintain its witness."

So the church stepped out in a bold move to take the orthodox gospel into an unorthodox setting. It booked the Men's Grill of Carson, Pirie, and Scott restaurant in the Loop, with a capacity of 600, and began to pray. The church asked the Lord to fill the grill for three nights, but not simply with Christians. Each Christian had to bring a non-Christian friend.

The *Chicago Daily News,* in a article entitled "Pastor Builds a Flock in Loop Meetings," described the scene:

> There were about 350 of them, heads bowed, praying in a department store dining room.
>
> The monthly dinner meeting of the "Moody Church in the Loop," while not formal service, had the element of worship throughout.
>
> "We have no right to expect people to come and listen to us," said the Rev. Alan Redpath, "unless first of all we show we're interested in them and are willing to meet them outside the walls of the church."

The format of these events: a dinner, good music, two brief testimonies, and a straightforward gospel message. Sample subjects: "Why Doesn't God Do Something?" "How to Overcome Pressures," "The Secret of a Happy Life."

Excerpts from Redpath's diary give a glimpse of the results:

April 23: "First meeting in Carson, Pirie, Scott & Co. Men's Grill. Total 311 present, probably about half non-Christians. Every evidence of the Holy Spirit having worked in power that evening. We had a real consciousness of Moody Church as a whole being in action and on the attack for God and for souls. This could well be the beginning of a new day for Moody Church in evangelism.

April 30: "Follow-up meeting at our house for those under 40."

May 7: "Another follow-up meeting at the home for those over 40."

May 28: "Second meeting at Carson's Grill. Almost 300. Half strangers to the gospel."

By fall the church had planned still another outreach and was in touch with a large number of its restaurant guests, many of them people of good social position but without any previous knowledge of the gospel.

January 25, 1959: Redpath's Sunday morning sermon topic: "How Can I Get a Christian Wife?"

March 24, 1959: "Attended the WGN television studio together with a section of the choir and we prepared a video-tape which will appear over Channel 9 on Sunday, April 12. One of the largest channels in Chicago ... but ... it is not an easy assignment to preach the Word to a few cameramen in a television studio!

September 11, 1959: "It was my privilege to speak yesterday at the installation service of my very dear friend, Stephen Olford, in his new pastorate at Calvary Baptist Church, New York City. I gave the charge to the minister and Dr. Billy Graham gave the charge to the congregation." Olford, also from England, had succeeded Redpath at an earlier church. The two could identify with each other on several fronts. "I know something of what is involved," Redpath wrote, "in the adjustment to life in a new country and the ministry in a metropolitan church in a large city."

"The next ten years will be the most critical in the history of Moody Church," Redpath told his congregation late in 1959. "We must face the challenge of a new constituency."

The crisis was underscored in an article by Redpath called "Mission Field on Our Doorstep—The Challenge of 1960":

> We have faced some immense problems with the steady drift of people to outer suburban areas—an exodus not forseen when our church building was erected thirty-five years ago. Yet some of the living conditions in homes in the immediate area of the church have been disgraceful, and it is high time that this rehabilitation took place.
>
> On the south side of the church a very fine new building is now being erected—a savings bank—which will occupy practically the entire space from Clark to LaSalle Street on North Avenue. Then for about a mile south of the church both on Clark and LaSalle Streets, you find wholesale demolition in progress.
>
> The ultimate completion of the whole rehabilitation plan will see Moody Church situated in the very heart of one of the finest inner-suburban areas of the whole city, with thousands of new families presenting a tremendous evangelistic opportunity.

The church even at that time had made some initial attempts to reach out to the new populace moving in. Callers used the telephone to establish initial contact, then tried to follow up with a personal call. Without a telephone call it was virtually impossible to gain entrance to a high rise apartment, and even then it proved extremely difficult. Apartment security totally eliminated cold calling.

For a time the blocks just to the south of Moody Church took on the appearance of a bombed-out area, until towering new apartments began to rise. An article in the *Chicago Daily News* (12 November 1960) vividly described the scene:

> A half-razed Near North slum has become one of the hottest pieces of real estate in the country, almost overnight. Developers are hovering around in platoons, waiting for the Chicago Land Clearance Commission, a public urban renewal agency, to put the land on sale. It runs in a strip along Clark and LaSalle streets, from Division to North, and is known as the North-LaSalle project. A year ago it was a jumble of weary old buildings, wretched tenements and small stores. Now many of the buildings are down and others are going fast. They will be replaced by sixteen hundred high-rise apartments.
>
> What makes the project so intriguing to real estate men is that it lies directly west of the Near North Gold Coast, and that the land will go at a knocked-down price. It is bound to become a westward arm of the plush neighborhood.

"We will be located right in the heart of one of the finest inner suburbs of any city of America," said Redpath. "Moody Church, known all over the world as a fundamental stronghold, will become one of the most strategically-placed churches in the country."

Meanwhile, more than 100,000 people, said a city survey, already lived within an eight-block radius of Moody Church.

But what would it take to get more of these people into the church? It would not happen, church leaders knew, automatically. For the majority of this populace, life-style did not include church—or at least an evangelical one.

For years, Moody Church had reached out to the surrounding neighborhood with its vacation Bible school and had taken the gospel into adjacent Lincoln Park in the summertime. Those traditions continued.

The Sunday evening outdoor service at six o'clock on the steps of the Lincoln monument, just to the east of the church, was described in an article by then associate pastor Bill Leslie:

> Hours of the vesper service, by permission of the Chicago Park District, are 6-6:45. The choir joins. Several hundred rally to an old fashioned hymn sing which begins each meeting. Some are on the way to the North Avenue Beach. Others are just relaxing in the park. We take enough hymnbooks for all and sing with an old pump organ. The church choir backdrops the meeting. Several of the Moody Church family, young and old, give testimony. We give out literature. After the close, some of the visitors make their way to Moody Church for the evening service. Over the years, no disturbances have marred the outreach.

More brief excerpts from the *Moody Church News* follow.

Summer 1960: The Redpaths tour India and other lands. The summer pulpit line-up in Redpath's absence, as usual, is a strong one: Moody Bible Institute's William Culbertson; Walter Wilson of Kansas City; J. Allen Fleece; Richard Seume; Harold Ockenga of Park Street Church, Boston; Paul Rees; former pastor Frank Logsdon; Wheaton College president V. Raymond Edman; Barrington College's Howard Ferrin; and Vance Havner.

October 1960: The church bids farewell to associate pastor Eric Crichton, who leaves to take a church in Toronto.

The cosmopolitan influx into the Moody Church neighborhood had triggered growing tensions. For decades the church had operated an integrated Sunday school, but it had no black members. In early 1961 a prominent article in the *Chicago Daily News* reported, "Moody Church Here Admits 3 Negroes."

"We are grateful for this milestone for Moody Church," the article quoted Redpath, who stressed that the congregation hoped to avoid making a "sensational" issue of the event. "We are interested in doing something that is right before God," said Redpath, "without stirring up emotional tensions." He said the step was taken "in the context of the surrounding neighborhood soon to be rehabilitated" and with the view of "greeting all who desire to come, regardless of race."

Meanwhile, the Elm LaSalle Bible Church, which Moody Church had planted in 1936 as an outgrowth of its Italian Mission, reached out to the ethnic crowd surrounding its own neighborhood down the street. Not all on the Moody Church board at the time were comfortable with its avantegarde social emphasis, which included a major tutoring program, coffee house, and pool tables. As tensions arose between the two churches, Redpath tried to calm the waters. The Elm LaSalle Church, however, drew widespread acclaim in the press, and Gospel Films produced *The Heart Cannot Run* to tell the church's story. It eventually became independent of Moody Church.

June 1961. Houghton College in New York state confers the degree of Doctor of Divinity on Pastor Redpath.

August 1961. Redpath preaches at the Church of the Open Door in Los Angeles. When its pastor, J. Vernon McGee, asks all those associated with Moody Church to stand, at least thirty people rise to their feet. "I did not venture to ask," quipped Redpath later, "what they were all doing in Los Angeles."

September 1961: God lays on the heart of Pastor Redpath and others the desire to provide a Christian day school.

November 1961: In Africa, Guy Playfair, General Director Emeritus of the Sudan Interior Mission and one of Moody Church's long-supported missionaries, celebrates his fiftieth year on the mission field at age seventy-nine.

Then in March 1962 appeared this announcement:

> My dear Friends:
>
> It is with mixed feelings yet in the conviction of being in the will of God that I have tendered my resignation from the pastorate at Moody Church, having received and accepted a call to the pastorate at Charlotte Chapel, Edinburgh, Scotland. This is the church where Dr. Graham Scroggie and Dr. Sidlow Baxter had such outstanding ministries over a period of years and it presents a unique opportunity of witness in the heart of Scotland's capital city. . . .
>
> The normal period of our stay at Moody Church after having given notice of resignation would be three months, but by mutual agreement between the Board here and the Board at Charlotte Chapel we have arranged to continue our ministry until Sunday, October 21. This will enable us to ensure that the fruit of the Billy Grahan Crusade is conserved for the church and will also enable us to lead one more Mid-America Keswick Convention, the closing Sunday of which will mark the termination of our ministry amongst you. . . .
>
> We shall never forget the love and the prayers which have surrounded us and supported us during these nine years of ministry. We are indeed thankful that our departure is not brought about by any problems or unhappiness at the church, where we have been conscious of a very warm-hearted fellowship.

After almost a decade in Chicago, Redpath returned to his native England.

Left: Yale-educated R. A. Torrey, who pastored Moody Church from 1894 to 1906, while also holding large evangelistic crusades as far away as Australia. He later became dean of the Bible Institute of Los Angeles (now Biola University).
Below: Dwight L. Moody's street urchins in new suits (Moody in center, James Farwell in top hat). Abraham Lincoln once visited Moody's Sunday school class.

Right: Dwight L. Moody
takes friends and family
on a buggy ride at his
home in Northfield,
Mass., in 1895.
Below: Nearly three
quarter million people
turn out to hear Moody
in a series of sixty
meetings at London's
Agricultural Hall.

Left: A. C. Dixon, who followed Torrey as pastor of Moody Church from 1906 to 1911, came to Chicago from the pastorate of the widely known Ruggles Street Church in Boston. He left to pastor the historic Metropolitan Tabernacle in London, England, made famous by Charles Spurgeon.

Right: P. W. Philpott (1922-1929) led Moody Church in building its present brick edifice at Clark and LaSalle. One of Canada's foremost preachers, he once turned down a nomination to Canada's Parliament.

Right: The North Side Tabernacle, which Moody built after the great Chicago fire of 1871 destroyed the original Illinois Street Church (below).

Left: The Chicago
Avenue Church at
Chicago and
LaSalle, now the
site of Moody
Bible Institute's
bookstore and
Houghton Hall.
It was re-named
The Moody
Church in 1901,
after Moody's
death.
Below: An early
Founder's Week
celebration in Old
Moody Church.

Above:
A historic
prophetic Bible
conference at
Moody Church
in 1914.
Right: The Old
Moody Church,
shortly before
it was razed
in 1939.

Left: A high-level view of Moody Memorial Church from above Clark and LaSalle. Below: The church's main Clark Street frontage in 1933.

In this aerial view looking northeast toward Lake Michigan, Moody Memorial Church can be seen in the lower left center. The buildings of Carl Sandburg Village rise to its immediate southeast.

Upper left: Organ pipes and cathedral light.
Center: Church windows.
Lower right: Choir loft.
Award-winning photography by Terry Tasche.

Left: Moody Memorial Church under construction in 1925. The Moody Tabernacle built in 1915 by Paul Rader is partially demolished at left. Some of the billboards once surrounding three sides of the tabernacle can still be seen.
Below: The inside of Moody Church.

Top: Harry Ironside in the pulpit.
Above: Dr. William Culbertson,
president, of Moody Bible Institute,
during Founders Week in Moody Church.

Left: Dr. Harry Ironside in a contemplative pose.
Below: Three successive pastors of Moody Church pose: Dr. Alan Redpath (1953-1962), Dr. Warren Wiersbe (1971-1978), and Dr. George Sweeting (1966-1971).

Right: Billy Graham's songleader, Cliff Barrows, helps celebrate the growth of "Songs in the Night."

Below: The Executive Committee of
Moody Memorial Church.

Above: Joe Springer, George Beverly Shea,
Torrey Johnson, and Pastor Erwin Lutzer at a "Songs in the Night" celebration.

Right: Erwin Lutzer with his wife, Rebecca, and three daughters— Lynn, Lori, and baby Lisa.

Left: Pastor Lutzer in his study.

Moody Memorial
Church—"A Church
that could change the
city in a city
that could change
the world."

8

Interim Years
(1962-1966)

Moody Church moved toward its 100th Anniversary year in 1964 without a pastor, but that would not deter its centennial celebration. The church's renowned poetess, Avis B. Christiansen, teamed up with songwriter Harry Dixon Loes to give the church its centenary hymn:

> Through a hundred years of blessing,
> God, in goodness and in grace,
> Has revealed His mighty power
> In this sacred hallowed place.
>
> *Refrain:*
>
> A hundred years of blessing—
> To God be all the praise,
> Whose hand of love and mercy
> Has guided all our ways!
> And should the Saviour tarry
> Another century
> May we be found still trusting.
> And serving faithfully.
>
> Through a hundred years of blessing,
> Every need He has supplied;
> As the gospel has resounded
> From this Lighthouse, far and wide.
> Through a hundred years of blessing,
> God has brought us to this hour!
> Unto Him be all the glory
> For His wonder-working pow'r!

At the church's centenary kick-off dinner New Year's Eve, Carl Armerding likened Moody Church to a tree, firmly planted in the Lord Himself. "The winds of storm," he said, "may cause it to lose a few branches or to bend and break at times, but the roots hold firm."

Only weeks earlier, President John F. Kennedy had been assassinated in Dallas, and the times seemed uncertain. But the church chose as its centenary theme "Jesus Christ the Same Yesterday, and Today and Forever." God always reigns above history.

The neighborhood continued to change. Families with years in Moody Church continued to move to the suburbs. Subcultures of all sorts swarmed the area, and modern "cliff dwellers" began to move into the first newly-completed high-rise buildings of Carl Sandburg Village. As the church sought a new pastor, its constituency debated what kind of man he should be and what directions the church should take in the future.

Many expressed concern that more than 50 percent of the church's membership were more than sixty years of age. "Who holds the future of Moody Church?" one member asked pointedly during a New Years Eve panel discussion. "Are these questions only going to resolve themselves over a long, bitter struggle between the opinions of the saints who built and maintained this church over past years and the opinions of an impatient, discontented young element?"

That same centennial year, J. C. Pollock, a British evangelical Anglican, published a completely new account of the life of the church's founder, D. L. Moody, covering the evangelist's career both in the British Isles and in America. *Moody, A Biographical Portrait,* published by the Macmillan Company of New York, soon became somewhat of a classic among the many Moody biographies, the majority written in earlier years. One segment of his book detailed some of Moody Church's early history. Pollock's quote of a letter sent by Moody to the Chicago Avenue church may have been timely:

> Of late you have been on my mind and heart far more than usual.... The only way any Church can get a blessing is to lay aside all difference, all criticism, all coldness and party feeling, and come to the Lord as one man; and when the Church lives in the power of the 13th chapter of First Corinthians I am sure that many will be added daily to the flock of God.

The pastoral search continued throughout 1964, while the church filled its pulpit with Harold Lindsell, Bruce Dunn, Wilbur M. Smith, William Culbertson, and a parade of other notables from the world of evangelicalism. Meanwhile, in 1964 the situation in Africa grew tense, and missionaries under the support of Moody Church were among those suddenly forced to evacuate from Congo.

Early in 1965, the church received word that well-known singing evangelist Homer Hammontree, beloved member of the church for more than fifty years and at one time assistant pastor and minister of music under P. W. Philpott, had been called home by his Lord in Tennessee. Exactly one week later the church also lost Harry Dixon Loes, composer of three thousand pieces of music—among them "Love Found a Way," "All Things in Jesus," and "Blessed Redeemer." Loes had been a part of the Moody Church fellowship for nearly seventy years, and there in its Sunday school in 1895 had invited the Lord Jesus into his heart at age five.

In September of 1965 evangelist George Sweeting filled the pulpit. Meanwhile, David R. Mains accepted the position of associate pastor. In mid 1966 the church extended a call to Sweeting. The church had finally found its senior pastor.

9

George Sweeting:
The Building Years
(1966-1971)

George Sweeting, who followed Redpath as pastor of Moody Church, could point to an indirect Dwight L. Moody heritage.

His Scottish father was converted and influenced through Bethany Hall in Glasgow, a ministry that resulted from the D. L. Moody evangelistic meetings in the British Isles a century ago. Sweeting's wife, Hilda, was also of European stock. Both grew up in the Hawthorne Gospel Church in Hawthorne, New Jersey. Both came to Moody Bible Institute in the early 1940s.

The Moody graduation class of 1945, to no one's surprise, chose George Sweeting as its men's speaker. Later at Gordon College, in Massachusetts, he graduated as president of his class.

For a decade as a traveling evangelist and artist, he spoke not only in churches and youth rallies in this country but also to thousands of servicemen on bases around the world. As head of Sweeting Crusades, his message echoed the theme "Christ is the answer" in many of Germany's refugee camps and in West Berlin's high schools during the postwar years.

When the oldest of his four sons became a teenager, Sweeting took the pastorate of the inner-city Madison Avenue Baptist Church of Paterson, New Jersey. He had already served two New Jersey churches early in his career, one as associate pastor of his home church. Five years in the heart of Paterson seasoned George Sweeting for the Moody Memorial Church of Chicago.

When he accepted the call in 1966, church attendance had declined to a low ebb. The congregation had been without a senior pastor for three years.

Sweeting would have to help the church rebuild. The hard-to-reach neighborhood ranged from the cloistered high-rise apartments of Sandburg Village to the counter-culture of Old Town just two blocks west. But Sweeting went to work on his goals and long-range plan. Before long the church began to turn around, and attendance climbed.

Before evening services, Sweeting often mingled with the crowd, getting to know people individually. The warmth of his personality would soon penetrate to every part of the large auditorium.

"Got the joy?" he would ask, bouncing into the church office. And because enthusiasm is contagious, it soon reflected in others.

The church promptly renovated Philpott Hall on the third floor as its new center for teenagers and scheduled Word of Life evangelist Jack Wyrtzen for a gigantic Chicagoland youth crusade. In early 1967 the church bade farewell to its assistant pastor, David Mains, who assumed his own inner city pastorate, and later in the year welcomed James Gwinn as minister of Christian education.

Bill Bright, founder and executive director of Campus Crusade, opened a huge Lay Institute for Evangelism at the church in October. Setting the example, Sweeting and church young people conducted monthly Saturday night evangelistic rallies at the Great Lakes Naval Training Center on Lake Michigan's North Shore. It was not unusual to see nearly a thousand sailors in attendance and more than one hundred respond to the invitation.

Pastor Sweeting made clear his commitment to the inner city as a matter of conscience. "The city is here to stay," he said. "We cannot ignore, deplore, or flee it forever."

Evangelical Christians often equate their faith with nice people, blue skies, smiles and upper class goals. In rural America the Protestant is dominant—in fact, the conservative Protestant is dominant. Their attitudes and style of life set the tone for the whole society—the respectable standard—the American way, so to speak. But in the city the Protestant is a distinct minority. Jews and Jewish values are influential. Roman Catholics outnumber Protestants, run far bigger church programs.

The majority of evangelicals have long held an anti-city attitude, associating the city with Sodom and Gomorrah, scarlet women, crime and filth. This "anti-urban bias" has kept us from penetrating three great areas of our world: Hinduism, Islam, and the modern city. Somehow we must come to realize that this attitude is suicidal to the Church of Jesus Christ.

Is this what we find in the New Testament? The apostles concentrated their efforts in the throbbing cities of their day. Many of the epistles stand today as evidence of the importance of the cities after whom these letters are named. The environment was not easy or compatible with the revolutionary new values introduced by the disciples in Christ.

Ephesus, located at the mouth of the Cayster River, was notorious for its luxury and moral looseness. Diana was the chief object of worship; and opposition to the Gospel was fierce.

Corinth, with a population of 600,000, was the largest city in Greece. The Corinthians were particularly prone to sexual promiscuity; enjoyed dragging each other off to court over any little difference of opinion. The city seethed with a mass of merchants, philosophers, ex-soldiers and peddlers of vice.

Rome, the metropolitan center of the Roman Empire, was riddled with perversions, court plots and murders. Its prosperity and immorality eventually brought its downfall.

These were the centers of life where Christianity took root and flowered throughout the known world. The apostles went neither to the fringes of the towns nor to the tents of the migrants. They saw no future for the Gospel in isolation. They moved into the heart of the teeming cities—into the synagogues, the market places, the busy streets.

We at Moody Church are thrilled to be located in the heart of our great city. We have been placed here by God, and by His soldiers of the past generation. Our roots go deep into the history of Chicago.

While respecting America's rural heritage and praising its mountains, oceans, and lakes, Sweeting challenged the common image of the city as only "a demonic assortment of hippies, prostitutes, junkies, gangsters, pool halls, slums, and vice dens.

What about the architectural beauty that lies in the old sections of the city? What about the fascinating ethnic atmosphere of whole sections of a city? What about the gold in the mire? What about the vigorous spirit in the children who have not yet been crushed by intolerance and greed? What about the beauty of the Gold Coast at dusk or the traffic arteries from Marina Towers? Or the interesting people walking down the avenue?

I like the cadence of the jackhammer. I like the sight of a huge crane hoisting steel beams into place. I like the flow of concrete, the clacking of a million heels on finished pavement. Here is action; here is life. In the crush of multitudes the power of the living Lord can still be sensed.

In early 1968 Sweeting brought "Songs in the Night" to Moody Church. The easy-listening, low-key, middle-of-the-night program, using top soloists and instrumentalists, had its origins in 1943 with Billy Graham, when he pastored the Village Church of Western Springs, a suburb west of Chicago. Graham hired a then obscure soloist, George Beverly Shea, for "Songs in the Night." In years to come the names of both Graham and Shea would become known worldwide.

"Songs in the Night" was already aired on forty-five stations in the United States and foreign countries. Moody Church set out to expand its outreach even further.

Sweeting's warm, conversational style fit well into the format of the broadcast, and listeners responded. Its late evening air time caught the lonely night travelers and many who would not otherwise be reached by a church. The program injected Moody Church directly into missionary radio. A listener in Kingston, Jamaica, wrote, "I was tuned to Trans World Radio ... and there I heard your program. It has changed my life."

Within weeks "Songs in the Night" was picked up by other stations, including Newark, New Jersey; Madison, Wisconsin; and North Pole, Alaska.

In 1968 the Fleming H. Revell Publishing Company released Sweeting's book "And the Greatest of These," an exposition of 1 Corinthians 13. And Moody Youth Camp changed its name to Camp MoYoCa, to give it more of an Indian flair.

That year Sweeting also introduced a Founder's Day fall "Homecoming," on the church's 105th anniversary. "It has long been felt that Moody Church's rich history would be of interest to all," Sweeting explained. "And although the church has always enjoyed a share in Moody Bible Institute's Founder's Week," he said, "the membership is seldom made aware of its own wealth of leadership in the history of the evangelical world."

For the special occasion the church acquired voice recordings of D. L. Moody, Ira Sankey, and H. A. Ironside. The homecoming crowd heard Ironside deliver his famous sermon "Charge That to My Account," which appears in the back of this book. The church showed slides of Moody campaigns, the life of D. L. Moody, and previous Moody Church buildings. Sweeting also enlisted the assistance of Emma Moody Powell of East Northfield, Massachusetts, D. L. Moody's granddaughter.

The church established a new history center in Woolley Hall and called new attention to its Borden Library, between Woolley and Torrey Chapel. The library was named for the noted "Borden of Yale," a young man who, despite great wealth and status and comfortable home, set out as a missionary early in life but became ill and died while on the way to the field. But his example inspired countless others of his generation to give their lives to the foreign fields. Moody Church received a portion of his estate.

Long-time associate pastor Howard A. Hermansen resigned his full-time capacity in 1968, because of health reasons, but remained part-time and enjoyed a memorable night of special tribute. Donald H. Smith joined the staff as assistant pastor.

In 1969 the church held its first city-wide sunrise service in years, with internationally known lecturer and evangelist David W. Breese as speaker.

Meanwhile, from an upper room of the church, "Dial-A-Story" reached out by telephone to more than 400 children a day. Children dialed a three-minute recorded gospel message by WMBI's "Aunt Theresa," the station's pioneer in children's programming, whose name had become a household word to thousands of Chicago area children.

The ministry had been launched two years earlier by church member Chester Humphries, who asked Theresa Worman to do a few pilot tapes. Humphries transferred the tapes to a Code-a-Phone and then ran a small ad in the Personals column of a daily newspaper.

Early predictions were that maybe a few dozen a day would call in. In the first week, 1,100 calls were received, and the machine overheated and broke down. More phones were installed. Children called in for correspondence courses (known as the "Mailbox Club"). The work grew steadily. Interest spread to other American churches and even abroad, where Christians in Trinidad, Ireland, and Japan considered similar ministries.

By late 1969, Sweeting had been elected to Moody Bible Institute's Board of Trustees. "Songs in the Night" had equipped itself for stereo, and the church mapped plans for a neighborhood day care center. Canada's Ernest C. Manning, former premier of Alberta, highlighted the church's second annual Founder's Day. An outstanding Bible teacher and preacher, Premier Manning conducted the coast-to-coast Canadian "Back to the Bible Hour" broadcast throughout his twenty-eight years in government.

One day later Sweeting left for Glasgow, Scotland, to begin a week-long ministry throughout the British Isles. He then went on to Rome's coliseum, preached on Mars Hill, where the apostle Paul delivered his famous sermon, and took his first tour of the Holy Land. The church bade farewell to the Robert Carbaughs, who had served the Moody Church music program for eleven years, he as choir director, Helen as organist.

In a unique event early in 1970, some one hundred Jewish friends, including numerous rabbis, and one hundred Gentiles joined in the church's first "Adventure in Understanding" banquet. The program focused on the miracles taking place in modern Israel. Significantly, nearly a decade later when Neo-Nazis threatened to march through the heavily Jewish Chicago suburb of Skokie, Moody Bible Institute, under George Sweeting, protested with a full-page ad in the *Chicago Tribune*.

In February the church opened the doors of its Day Care Center, licensed for operation by the city of Chicago. It called Tom Streeter as assistant pastor in charge of youth and in May held its third annual "Songs in the Night" luncheon in the grand ballroom of Chicago's Marriott to help finance the growing radio ministry. A short time later its outreach topped 100 stations. Cliff Barrows, Billy Graham's teammate and songleader, highlighted the 1970 homecoming.

By 1971 Moody Church, under George Sweeting, had reversed its decline and had weathered Chicago's inner-city turmoil of the late 1960s. New horizons lay ahead, both for the church and for Sweeting. For in that year he resigned to accept the presidency of Moody Bible Institute, one mile south on LaSalle.

10

Warren Wiersbe:
The Songs-in-the-Night Years
(1971-1978)

With an unusual sense of the Holy Spirit's guidance, Moody Church in midsummer 1971 extended a call to Warren W. Wiersbe to serve as senior pastor. For ten years Wiersbe had been pastor of Calvary Baptist Church in Covington, Kentucky, a part of the Greater Cincinnati area. His church had just completed a new 2,000-seat sanctuary.

Earlier Wiersbe had served with Youth For Christ International, heading their literature division and editing *YFC Magazine* (now *Campus Life*). He had also pastored a church in East Chicago, Indiana, a blue-collar region where theology had to speak the language of the common man. An able preacher, teacher, and writer, Wiersbe graduated from Northern Baptist Seminary in Chicago. He had also studied at Indiana University and Chicago's Roosevelt University and in 1965 was awarded an honorary Doctor of Divinity degree by Tennessee Temple in Chattanooga.

A man with radio experience as well, Wiersbe promptly became the new voice on the Moody Church "Songs in the Night." Its outreach would soon climb to 200 stations. In late January 1972, at the Hilton Hotel in Washington, D.C., with many senators and congressmen present, the National Religious Broadcasters gave "Songs in the Night" a citation of honor.

As Wiersbe settled in, he paid tribute to his predecessor George Sweeting. "He built wisely and well. My task as pastor is that much easier because he did his job that much better." Added Wiersbe, "Hats off to the past, and coats off to the future!"

Among the church's major challenges ahead: the parking problem. The church enjoyed use of a parking area in the south end of Lincoln Park, a block to the north, but it was inadequate for church growth, or, for that matter, any special event—and Moody Church had many of them. Winter snows further complicated the problem.

Some of the church's younger generation, in particular, pushed ahead with high rise Bible studies. One convert from these groups told his story this way:

> A Christian friend suggested I visit his Bible class. I really don't know why I agreed to go. Whatever the reason, a few hours later we stood outside an apartment door. Before entering I felt it necessary to apologize to my friend for what I was sure would be my feelings after seeing a bunch of "goody-goody" Christians chirp praises to some "phantom." Four weeks later I gave my life to Christ.
>
> What made these people different? They were friendly, but so are bartenders. They seemed interested in my life, but so do people I've met at cocktail parties. There was something else in that apartment last spring, the love of our Lord Jesus Christ and the power of the Holy Spirit.

The music of Moody Church, as over the decades, continued to prove outstanding. The annual presentation of the "Messiah" continued to draw many from the Chicago "culture" crowd, not accustomed to hearing such fine music in an evangelical church. Daniel Majeske, gifted young concert-master of the Cleveland Orchestra—and an evangelical Christian—presented a fall violin concert. Guest artist Frank Boggs handled the Thanksgiving night concert, and John Innes played regularly at the Moody Church piano when he was not away with the Billy Graham crusades. The Moody Choir and Orchestra, with sixty singers and fifty-five players, presented the "Christmas Festival," which one described as "the most thrilling annual Christmas concert in the Chicago area." Meanwhile, the Moody Church choir cut a stereo record produced by RCA entitled "A New Song."

The church collected $550,000 in 1972 to finish the year in the black, handled more than 200,000 pieces of mail, and hired Warren Filkin as minister of visitation and adult ministries.

A sudden fuel crisis late in 1973 threatened to partially immobilize the church's forward momentum. Wiersbe cautioned that members not use it as an excuse to stay home but also advised doubling up. "Somehow it always pains me," he said, "to see a man drive up in an empty car." The church modified its calendar to minimize the number of evening trips to the church for committee meetings and encouraged use of the church's zone plan, which had assigned deacons and others to call on fellow members in their own postal zone, thus saving driving all over the city.

In 1974 Billy Graham, with George Beverly Shea, highlighted the church's thirtieth anniversary rally of "Songs in the Night." One listener flew all the way from Honolulu for the event. That year the church also launched the

Moody Church Hour, a delayed tape of the regular Sunday morning service. After a test on Moody Bible Institute's stations in East Moline and St. Petersburg, it was offered to other stations. By September it had cracked the Chicago market, a matter of special prayer, with placement on WEFM, one of Chicago's leading cultural FM radio stations.

At its annual meeting the church reported a membership of 1,489. Although other major metropolitan churches, especially in the South, could point to greater congregations, Moody Church could point to a major outreach across Chicago: the dual radio programs "Songs in the Night" and the new "Moody Church Hour"; the Day Care Center for preschool and kindergarten children; the Sunday school and bus ministry to neighborhood children; music ministry to the culturally oriented citizenry; Camp Moyoca with a summertime camping program; an active youth program for young people of high school and college age. Above all, the Word of God was preached week after week, and for this there could be no substitute.

Other traditions continued: the church's annual world missionary conference, its annual home missions conference, and the long-standing New England dinner.

When a visiting pastor asked, "How do you go about reaching a big city like Chicago?" Wiersbe answered him with a fourfold formula: the Word of God, prayer, friendliness, and music.

Although Wiersbe maintained Moody Church dignity, his humor and quick wit were no secret, either to the church or to thousands of young people to whom he had ministered in earlier years under Youth For Christ. That humor surfaced often, as the night the church's high schoolers at an Omega Club banquet pulled off a stirring rendition of "Trigger Mortis, Frontier Mortician," a comedy written by—yes—Pastor Wiersbe.

On the Sunday of the church's fiftieth anniversary in its building at Clark and LaSalle, Wiersbe spoke on "What mean these stones?" taken from the same text in Joshua 4 that P. W. Philpott chose for the building's dedication sermon a half century before:

> Joshua had the men of Israel erect two monuments, one in the midst of the Jordan, and the other on the bank of the Jordan. These two piles of twelve stones each—one seen and the other under the water—had a special meaning to Israel. They were reminders of what God had done. A new generation would arise that would not know Joshua or the other great men of the past, and the stones on the river bank would teach them and remind them of their heritage.
>
> The Moody Church today can learn from those two monuments. As a new generation looks at these buildings and asks, "What mean these stones?" we ought to be able to give a clear answer to the glory of God.
>
> Joshua was wise in his choice of material for the monuments, for to an

Israelite a rock was the most substantial thing he knew. In fact, he even compared God to a Rock! A river is about the most changing thing he knew, for a river is never the same, always moving.

It seems to me that we have three kinds of churches today. We have *rock churches* that resist change and have no intention of changing. They are like citadels, and I'm afraid they are not ministering to the needs of people today. Other churches are *river churches*—ever changing. They are like chameleons! Whatever new thing comes along, they grab it and put it into their program. The citadel church has a great past but no future, and the chameleon church has neither past nor future! Both are destined to die.

Our church must be a *creative* church, one that honors the past but is willing to change to minister to the present. We cannot live on past blessings or past victories. We want to remember the past to the glory of God, but we also need to *bury the past.* There is a tendency among the people of God to worship the past and think only of "the good old days." The past can be the enemy of the present.

In a poem that paid tribute to the past but set the tone for the future, Moody Church poetess/hymnwriter Avis B. Christiansen wrote "Fifty Golden Years":

> What a glad date to remember!
> 'Twas the eighth day of November
> Fifty blessed golden years ago,
> That our Moody congregation
> Gathered for the dedication
> Of this House of God we all love so.

> After months of prayerful planning,—
> Faithfully all problems scanning,
> Seeking daily guidance from Above,
> We beheld here in its glory
> By God's grace the "finished story,"
> Gift of His eternal bounteous love.

> 'Twas with awe and admiration
> That our joyous congregation
> Viewed the scene with mingled joy and tears,
> Praising God for His provision,
> And the glorious fruition
> Of our dreams and hopes through all the years.

> E'er since that momentous hour
> God has shown His grace and power
> Through each forward step along our way,
> And has opened His good treasure
> Unto us in fullest measure
> As we've sought to follow day by day.

Fifty years of joy and blessing,
We've experienced, confessing
His dear Name unto a needy race,—
Telling o'er and o'er the story
How our Lord left Heaven's glory
To redeem the world in matchless grace.

On the Rock of Ages founded,
In His Word securely grounded,
We have kept the Faith through all the years,
And by grace we will not falter,
Nor our glorious message alter
Till our blessed Lord at last appears.

In 1976 Moody Church stood ready to celebrate another anniversary, the nation's Bicentennial. Crowds filled the church on May 14 to hear the Moody Choir present "Festival Americana," chosen as one of the official American Revolution Bicentennial events in Chicago. The program included American masterworks, settings of American hymns and gospel songs, and unique arrangements of several patriotic selections. It was a once-in-a-lifetime experience, and for many people it was their introduction to Moody Church. Then followed another musical extravaganza—sacred and patriotic—on July 4.

The church set a 1976 goal of $100,000 for renovation projects on its building and later another $150,000 to remodel Sankey Auditorium for much needed Sunday school space. The "Here's Life America" campaign came to Chicago in November, with Moody Church one of the city's "main training camps." The church joined 350 other Chicago area evangelical churches in a mass telephone campaign to reach as many Chicagoans as possible with the gospel. Moody Church assigned 150 workers to a bank of twenty-one telephones, calling through the evening hours for three straight weeks.

Membership by 1978 had eased up to 1,569, not a dramatic gain, but respectable. Although crowds often filled the 4,000-seat sanctuary for special events, the balcony remained empty for most regular services. "Our growth has been slow but steady," Wiersbe noted. "How I wish we had a full auditorium!" But the words and wisdom of beloved veteran preacher Vance Havner carry insight here: "It is not the business of the pastor to fill the church," he said. "It is the business of the pastor to fill the pulpit." That Wiersbe did well.

The church undertook new ministries: an outreach to singles, and the distribution of Wiersbe's messages on cassette tape. Some 13,000 tapes were distributed in one year. "Songs in the Night" nudged 250 stations, an all-time high. In 1978 the Moody Choir released no fewer than four albums on the commerical market, one with Word Records ("The Lord Whom We Love"), the others on Zondervan's Singcord and Singspiration labels ("Rhapsody in Praise," "All Hail the Power," and John Peterson's cantata "No Greater Love.") Few church choirs can attain the professionalism to record for a market outside their own church congregation, let alone for two major recording companies—in the same year!

In May 1978, Wiersbe submitted his resignation as senior minister for "a wider ministry of Bible conference teaching and writing" but remained a member of Moody Church. Today he is general director and radio voice of the far reaching Back to the Bible Broadcast, Lincoln, Nebraska.

Moody Church began immediately to search for Wiersbe's replacement. In the interim, the congregation reeled in shock when assistant pastor Donald H. Smith died of injuries sustained in an automobile accident. An able administrator and accomplished musician, Smith had built "Songs in the Night" from 61 stations to more than 230 in his ten years on staff.

Months later the church brought in Joseph A. Springer, United States director of World Missionary Fellowship and long-time radio missionary with HCJB in Quito, Ecuador, to succeed Smith. And for the 1978 fall quarter, the church chose Erwin Lutzer, an associate professor at Moody Bible Institute, as pulpit supply.

11

Erwin Lutzer:
The Discipling Years
(1980—   )

Erwin Wesley Lutzer was born on a farm near Regina, Saskatchewan. Since the age of eight he had a desire to preach, though he pictured himself as an evangelist, not a pastor, primarily because of his fascination with the life and ministry of Billy Graham.

"I would listen to the Hour of Decision on Sunday," he recalls, "and preach as though I were Billy Graham while riding on the tractor or going to school."

His parents had both come from Germany in the late 1920s but met for the first time while attending the same church in Canada. Gustav had accepted Christ in Germany, but Wanda was converted during evangelistic services held in a small church. They knew each other only two weeks before they were married. From the beginning they chose to make Jesus Christ the head of their home. Prayer, they believed, was the single most important ingredient in the lives of their children.

The last of five children, Erwin was shy by nature. When company arrived, a brother or sister often had to pull him from under the bed. But in high school he outgrew this shyness.

Although he had heard the gospel as a child, he had no assurance of salvation. He would pray almost every evening asking Christ to come into his life, but nothing seemed to happen. In fact, he began to wonder if, for some reason, he was not ordained to eternal life. But at the age of fourteen, his parents explained the need simply to accept Christ in faith, whether he felt different or not. After a time of prayer with his parents, he never doubted his salvation again.

Erwin Lutzer preached his first sermon while in the twelfth grade at the Christian high school he attended. On Saturday evenings he often went witnessing with other high school friends, giving out tracts and sharing the gospel. These experiences confirmed his conviction that some day he would preach.

During high school, on his own initiative he began to memorize Scripture. When he enrolled at Winnipeg Bible College, he promised himself that he would not graduate until he had memorized all twenty-one chapters of the gospel of John. After working on this book for three years, he recited it in two hours and twenty minutes—five months ahead of schedule. Later he memorized all of Romans, Ephesians, Philippians, and Hebrews. Often he reviewed what he learned while plowing a field or harvesting a crop. One day he recited Scripture for four hours and thirty minutes—without repeating himself.

In the mid-sixties Franklin Logsdon came to the Christian and Missionary Alliance Church in Regina, where the Lutzer family attended. Erwin attended every evening and was impressed with Logsdon's ability to teach entire books of the Bible from memory. Little did Erwin realize that fifteen years later he also would paster the Moody Church, as had Logsdon (1950–51), and that he would welcome Logsdon back to the pulpit on June 24, 1984.

After graduating from Bible college, Erwin Lutzer attended Dallas Theological Seminary, where he met Rebecca Hickman, a student at Dallas Bible College. They met in church but did not begin a serious relationship until after Lutzer's graduation in 1967. Two years later they were married.

He taught at the Briercrest Bible Institute in Canada for three years, then brought his wife to Chicago in the summer of 1970. Lutzer had been accepted for Ph.D studies at a university on the east coast, but a Moody Bible Institute professor encouraged him to attend a local university. They have lived in Chicago ever since.

In the fall of 1971 Lutzer, with the intent of teaching in seminary, began studies in philosophy at Loyola University. But after preaching for several months at the Edgewater Baptist Church, on Chicago's North Shore, he was asked to stay on as pastor. The Lutzers remained there for nearly six years (1971–1977). He resigned to give more time to his university studies during the summer and also to teach at Moody Bible Institute.

Edgewater Baptist Church held a farewell for the Lutzers in March 1977. In Erwin's words, "We woke up the next Sunday without a church to attend." So on April 3, they decided to drive down to the Moody Church just once—to hear Pastor Wiersbe, with whom he sometimes met for prayer.

The family did not attend Sunday school that morning. Erwin dropped off Rebecca and their three daughters at the church and began looking for a parking place. A moment later someone pulled out of a space on LaSalle Street, and Lutzer was able to park the car directly across the street from the church. He walked into the lobby looking for Rebecca. Pastor Wiersbe came past with his topcoat on.

"I put my hand on his shoulder," says Lutzer, and asked, "What are you doing here? You have only ten minutes before the service."

Wiersbe replied, "Erwin, I'm sick. I'm on my way home. Will you preach for me this morning?"

Lutzer agreed to do so.

Dr. Wiersbe introduced him to the church staff. Lutzer took a few moments to write down the outline of a message he had preached previously, "The Renewing of the Mind."

As he stood on the platform that morning he said in his heart, "Lord, if they ever call me to this church, I'll say yes," though he didn't seriously think that would ever happen. That morning he spoke with great freedom. On the way home in the afternoon they stopped at a gas station and asked for $5 worth of gas; the attendant inadvertently gave them $8 worth instead but charged them for only $5. "We not only attended the right church," Rebecca said to Erwin that afternoon, "but also the right gas station."

When Wiersbe resigned in 1978, the church asked Lutzer to become its stated pulpit supply. He filled that role for a year and a half, as Moody Church sought a permanent pastor and even interviewed several candidates. When anyone suggested that God may have already supplied a pastor in the person of Erwin Lutzer, Erwin declined any official discussion of the matter. "I wanted the church to investigate as many others as possible," he told Byrl Vaughan, chairman of the board of elders and head of the pastoral search committee. In his heart he believed he would eventually be called for the position, though he was awed by the thought. Rebecca was hesitant about his taking on such a big responsibility, especially because of their relatively young age and their small children.

But when the church finally extended the call, she was as enthusiastic as her husband about their new ministry.

The vote of the executive committee was unanimous. On November 28, 1979, the congregation voted to accept the recommendation of the executive committee. Lutzer officially began his pastorate January 1, 1980.

God's call to Moody Church was confirmed in many ways, Lutzer believes today. It was no accident, he is convinced, that a man pulled his car onto LaSalle that morning at precisely the right moment. If Lutzer had entered the church lobby a minute later, or a minute earlier, he would not have seen Pastor Wiersbe. The unanimous vote, coupled with the fact he had already preached at the church for nearly eighteen months, helped confirm his thinking.

Lutzer was installed as senior pastor on January 20, with former pastor

George Sweeting, now president of Moody Bible Institute, and Dr. John Walvoord of Dallas Theological Seminary presiding. Lutzer responded by reflecting on the honor that God had given him. "There are no preachers in my family; there is nothing in my background to suggest that I should ever have the privilege of serving as pastor of this historic church."

That day he wrote in his diary: "This day marks a highlight in my life. The installation service was beautiful and so was the weather. The temperature was in the 40's without a flake of snow on the ground. May God give me the grace to minister with blessing. Lord, I am yours for whatever you desire."

By the time Erwin Lutzer was installed as pastor at the age of thirty-eight, he was already known to many beyond Moody church through his writing ministry. In 1971 he had published his first book, *The Morality Gap*, a philosophical work defending biblical morality against the onslaughts of situation ethics. Other books that focused on Christian living followed. *How In This World Can I Be Holy?* and *Failure: The Back Door to Success* were published in 1972 and 1973 respectively. Then came *Flames of Freedom*, the story of the Canadian revival that swept western Canada in the early seventies. He followed these with *How to Say No to a Stubborn Habit* and *Living with Your Passions*, the latter written after coming to Moody Church. More recently he has penned *Twelve Myths That Could Destroy America*, a book that deals with the church in our increasingly humanistic society. He has written ten books in all, plus numerous magazine articles.

In October of his first year Lutzer preached a series of messages on revival. On October 5, more than two hundred people responded to the invitation to get fully right with God and in faith die to self-will. Yet for all the encouragement he received, the first year at the church had been difficult. Lutzer wrote in his diary, "Dear Father. Sometimes I feel as if you have called me without giving me the ability to fulfill your calling. You have been precious through the rough spots, but I need grace to bear the many burdens and responsibilities and minister with power."

When he came to the church, Lutzer told the congregation that he believed the preaching ministry should be supplemented with specific training sessions for evangelism, discipleship, and pastoral care. "A large church," he says, "must be personalized."

In the fall of 1981 the church formed "Oasis" groups in different parts of the city. The dictionary defines an oasis as "a fertile or green area in a desert region." To many the city of Chicago seems like an impersonal desert. People desperately need a "fertile area" where they can share and grow. Although people join an Oasis voluntarily, their decision involves a commitment to pray, study, and communicate on a regular basis.

Successful as these groups were, the church leadership believed it was necessary to have a shepherding program that would encompass the entire membership. So care groups were formed throughout the city—open only to Moody Church members. A lay shepherd is in charge of each group, and he reports to a regional shepherd on any problems that might arise. The groups are required to meet periodically for fellowship and to sustain a mutual caring ministry. The greatest challenge is to find qualified leadership. Significant benefits have come to those who have established new friendships and a sense of accountability.

Navigator 2:7 groups have been of great help in discipling those who are willing to make the commitment to personal study and interaction. Up to thirty are involved in the program, some at advanced levels of study.

Lutzer believes that if Moody Church is to grow, it will happen through effective evangelism. Because parking near the church is limited, those who drive to the church need a high level of dedication. But Lutzer insists that the church's basic roots must be planted in the neighborhood.

In 1981 the pastor of singles and evangelism launched a program called REECH (Reaching through Evangelism Explosion Chicago). In one three-month period alone more than twenty people made a first-time profession of faith in Jesus Christ. The program continues to bear much fruit.

The church's radio ministries have continued. The popular Sunday evening program "Songs in the Night" now has new voices. Joe Springer, formerly of HCJB, Quito, Ecuador, joined the Moody staff to direct the radio ministry. Four thousand letters poured into the church office during the first quarter of 1980. WMBI, now on satellite, carries "The Moody Church Hour" every Sunday morning, and it is picked up by other stations around the country. It is estimated that the program is released eighty times each week in various parts of the United States. Joe and Betty Springer returned to Quito in 1984 to teach in a missionary school, and Moody Church radio now reaches out under new personnel.

Dr. Lutzer believes that the key to effective church leadership is the unity and commitment of the pastoral staff. "I'm so grateful that God has sent us a good team," he says. "We meet together every Friday morning for prayer and the coordination of our ministries. I look forward to it because of the fellowship, discussion, and planning we do."

Two auxiliary ministries of the church, both begun under previous pastors, remain strong: Camp Moyoca and the Day Care Center. Success is due to the leadership of those who are in charge. Most of the camp work is handled by volunteers who have given thousands of hours to its program and upkeep. Each week during the camp season young people accept Christ as Savior and grow in faith. The Day Care Center impacts not only the children of the neighborhood but their parents as well.

Now Moody Church has initiated a new ministry called "Women in the Working World." Working women attend a monthly luncheon and enjoy a program customized for their needs, including how to be a Christian on the job. A fall women's seminar includes workshops for the working woman.

In 1983 the church announced the launching of "Operation Nehemiah," an ambitious project to catch up on deferred maintenance and to refurbish the church for the future. The Operation Nehemiah Committee assembled a list of more than thirty projects that would need attention in order to bring the building to acceptable standard. Included was the renovation of Woolley Hall for use as a visitors' lounge. The total cost of the projects was estimated at more than a million dollars.

Associate Pastor Bruce Jones explains that, once completed, the church building should not need any major repairs for the next twenty to thirty years. Phase one of Operation Nehemiah began in the summer of 1983 with the painting, carpeting, and redecorating of the auditorium. Scaffolding rose to its sixty-eight foot ceiling and remained there for three weeks while workmen finished the project. Masonry repair and cleaning, as well as new concrete deck stairs, were also completed. Thanks to the gift of a large estate, the church also completed roof repair (at a cost of $200,000) and installation of new windows.

In September 1983, the church held an Operation Nehemiah banquet at the Chicago Marriot Hotel, with Cliff Barrows of the Billy Graham team as keynote speaker and Myrtle Hall as soloist. The congregation was encouraged to make a three-year faith promise to fund the renovations. To date contributions have totalled more than $300,000. The church premiered a new multi-media entitled "Moody Church—The Church That Can Change the City in a City That Could Change the World."

Is such a challenge realistic? Dr. Lutzer believes it is , but only if the church is prepared to return to the pattern revealed in the book of Acts. The early Christians left the city of Jerusalem when their lives were threatened, but they were not intimidated. They witnessed wherever they went. Satan tried to use persecution to blow out the flame, but instead he blew the fire over the whole landscape. Christians bore fruit wherever God happened to plant them.

In October 1983, Ray Bakke conducted a seminar at Moody Church on how to reach the city with the gospel. His basic thesis: If you can penetrate the city, you can penetrate the world. The potential is there.

With such vision in mind, Moody Church launched in the fall of 1985 a program entitled "Win Your World for Christ." Bruce Jones explained the strategy to the congregation. He asked each one to ask God to reveal those neighbors and friends whose names should be written on a prayer list and consistently remembered in intercessory prayer. Then he offered instruction on how to build bridges to the unsaved world. The potential is awesome: if 1,000 believers participate and each were to choose 8 unsaved friends, 8,000 people would be lovingly confronted with the gospel in a year. The program has just begun, but initial enthusiasm is running high.

With the revitalization of the inner city and the encouragement of a revived interest in personal evangelism, the present leadership of Moody Church is praying that some of the greatest days of ministry may still lie ahead. To be "the church that can change the city in a city that could change the world" is the challenge that lies before them.

12

The Future Years
(1985 . . . ?)

Moody Church is one of the world's most famous churches. From the United States to Great Britain and the Continent, and even as far away as China, the name of D. L. Moody and the Moody Church is known to Christians. World famous evangelists and Bible conference speakers have come to preach at Moody Church with a sense of its history and appreciation for the opportunity to stand behind its pulpit.

The stability and strength of Moody Church is found not only in its rich heritage but more so in the unchangeable foundation of Jesus Christ who is "the same yesterday, today and forever." For more than 120 years the church's faith has been rooted in the Word of God, which lives and abides forever. Its pulpit has always proclaimed the gospel—that Jesus Christ died upon the cross for sinners, who can be saved by putting their confidence in Him alone. Over the years thousands have come to Christ through the church's influence.

The spiritual heritage of Moody Church is rich. Its pastors and people have left a legacy of world-wide influence. Its contribution to the cause of missions alone is unusual. Mission leaders from among its ranks have fulfilled the great commission around the world. Consider again just these few examples:

Fredrik Franson, the "gun powder preacher" who went to Europe with a passionate zeal and founded what is today known as TEAM (The Evangelical Alliance Mission).

Borden of Yale, who accepted Christ at Moody Church at the age of seven and gave $1 million dollars to missions before he died on the mission field at the age of twenty-seven.

Peter Deyneka, saved under the ministry of Paul Rader, who went on to establish the Slavic Gospel Association, which ministers to thousands behind Iron Curtain countries in Europe.

Herbert Hudson Taylor, son of the founder of China Inland Mission, who was influenced by the ministry of Moody Church and served for many years as a missionary in China.

Guy Playfair, who became the second general director of the Sudan Interior Mission.

Today, Moody Church supports 131 missionaries in various mission fields of the world.

The pulpit of the Moody Church has been one of the strongest in the world. Famous preachers from Europe (G. Campbell Morgan, Gipsy Smith, and Alan Redpath, to name a few) have stood before thousands gathered at the church to hear the Word of God. There are Christian school presidents who at one time were either pastors or pulpit supply in the church— men like Charles Blanchard of Wheaton and R.A. Torrey and George Sweeting of the Moody Bible Institute. Many of its pastors have not only been powerful pulpiteers but have also used the pen to proclaim the Word— men like Ironside, Wiersbe, and Lutzer.

But all the past is prologue. No church, not even Moody Church, can rest upon its past. Each new generation brings its own fresh challenge to a church that must not alter its message but must be flexible in changing its methods to reach a new world at its doorstep. When D. L. Moody began his ministry he was led of God to reach the ragged street children of Chicago. As he rode his Indian pony he attracted children and had them meet in a church or a rented bar room for Sunday school. Later he built an evangelical network to reach 2 million people during the 1883 Chicago World's Fair. Later men such as A. C. Dixon wrote articles in the *Chicago Daily News* to evangelize its readers. During the 1933 World's Fair 50,000 copies of the book "The Reason Why" were distributed, and 300,000 people came to hear Harry Ironside teach the simple truths of the Bible.

During the suburban exodus of the late fifties, Alan Redpath stressed neighborhood visitation. He organized evangelistic dinners in a Loop restaurant, where hundreds of non-churched people were reached with the gospel. George Sweeting used direct mail and local evangelistic rallies. And now the church today must find the methods most appropriate to share the same unchanging message.

Since the Chicago fire in 1871 the face of the city has obviously changed. But even in more recent decades the area surrounding Moody Church has undergone urban renewal. Old neighborhoods with single family dwellings have been replaced by high-rise complexes in which thousands of people may be found at essentially the same address.

Not only has the face of the neighborhood changed, but so also has the family structure. The new neighbors of Moody Church are primarily business and professional people, many of whom are single. A few decades ago the Sunday school at Moody Church was 2/3 children and only 1/3 adults. Today it is 2/3 adults and 1/3 children. Perhaps almost half of those who attend Moody Church are single, though they span virtually every age category.

Moody Church is now in the midst of a mission field larger than some small countries. Situated in the nation's third largest city, it has thousands upon thousands of unchurched people on its front doorstep. It is located strategically and geographically in a position to confront this new generation with the gospel of Christ. The 1985 strategy to "win your world for Christ" is a small step toward the challenge "to be the church that can change the city in the city that could change the world."

This awesome mandate cannot be accomplished by looking to the past. Nor can it become a reality simply by having an outstanding pulpit ministry, important though that may be. The church must rise to the challenge of a new day with the commitment of D. L. Moody who said:

> You have had enough of pulpit preaching. What we want now is hand to hand work. Personal effort, individuals going to people and pressing on them the claims of Christ.... Christians need to be involved in an evangelistic war of aggression.

By God's grace the leaders of Moody Church want it to become that kind of a church to face the challenges of tomorrow. D. L. Moody confronted a needy city with Jesus Christ. This flaming torch must be passed on to succeeding generations.

13

P. W. Philpott:

What Mean These Stones?

A Memorial Sermon

The following sermon, based on Joshua 4:21 and rich with insight into the life of Dwight L. Moody, was delivered on November 8, 1925, the Sunday on which the Moody Church dedicated its new 4,200-seat edifice at Clark and LaSalle.

It would appear that almost from the beginning of history man has perpetuated the memory of his heroes and his epoch-making events by piling together stones. We can trace the custom in the Bible as far back as Genesis 28. You will remember that we find recorded there the story of Jacob's wonderful vision of God in which God promised divine protection and provision. Jacob took the stones of that place and made a pillar, and anointing it with oil he called the name of it Bethel—the house of God.

That was indeed a worthy idea. To Jacob that spot would evermore be sacred. It was the place where he met God, and he did not wish to lose any part of the impression of so memorable an event.

The monument spoken of in the text was erected by Joshua and his hosts at Gilgal on the banks of the Jordan to commemorate the great deliverances God had wrought for His people Israel. They piled together stones not only because they remembered the goodness and mercy of Jehovah, but lest they and their children should forget.

So we, actuated by similar motives, have built a monument with which is associated hallowed memories and a history that is soul-thrilling and God-glorifying. In the years to come when men ask, "What mean these stones?" there will be a story to tell—a story of love and grace, a story of divine power and faithfulness, a story that will exalt our precious Lord as the Savior of all who believe.

First of all, the building is to stand as a memorial to one of Chicago's greatest citizens.

A few years ago one of the leading morning papers carried an editorial entitled "Chicago's Most Notable Citizen," and the man of whom it spoke was D. L. Moody. No other has ever succeeded in making Chicago so well and so favorably known as did that dear servant of God. But Mr. Moody was not provincial. He was not only Chicago's most famous citizen but one of the most widely-known men in the United States.

Professor Henry Drummond, the distinguished British scientist and theologian, in an article contributed to *McClure's Magazine* a few years ago, stated:

> Probably America possesses no more extraordinary personality. Not even among the most brilliant of her sons has any one rendered more stupendous or more enduring service to his country or his time. Whether estimated by the moral qualities which go to the making up of his personal character, or the extent to which he has impressed these on whole communities of men on both sides of the Atlantic, there is perhaps no more truly great man living than D. L. Moody.

Dr. John R. Mott wrote an article which appeared in the *American Magazine* about two years ago entitled "The Seven Greatest Men That I Have Known" in which he gave Mr. Moody first place.

Moody's ministry and vision were worldwide. He belonged to the whole human family. "His parish," as Wesley said, "was the world."

Last year in the British Isles they celebrated the Moody and Sankey Jubilee. For months the religious press carried editorials and leading articles on the ministry of this man who had turned hundreds of thousands from sin to the Savior and "whose fruit abides after many days."

D. L. Moody was more than an evangelist; he was an educator—an educator of the most practical and helpful kind.

It has often been stated that he was an uneducated man, but that is surely far from fact unless the term is used in the narrowest and most technical sense of the word. It is true that Moody was a man of one book, but oh, what a Book! "Profitable for doctrine, for reproof, for correction, for instruction in righteousness, that the man of God may be perfect, thoroughly furnished unto all good works." Moody surely believed that statement, and he himself was the best kind of demonstration of the accuracy of it.

The day following his death, the *Chicago Tribune* published a special article, part of which I would quote here:

From the time when he came to Chicago in 1856, a young man of nineteen—and crude and raw enough at that—he was an educator. The first thing he did was to begin to teach. Education in its way was then, as since then, the passion of his life. He began where he could and with whom he could. He began with the little ragamuffins on the street. He could not bear to think of them as having no other education than that which they were getting on the street. And if at the beginning he did not feel himself competent to teach them much, he got others to do the teaching while he created and managed the school. And that, in effect, is what he had been doing as an educator ever since.

As an evangelist his preaching was never mere appeal and exhortation. He always aimed to be instructive. In a supreme kind of way he took the Bible as his textbook. As a student he pored over it day and night. As an educator he taught it, in season and out of season. Nor did he disdain to get helpful ideas or to utilize the most pat and effective forms of statement from whatever sources. What the Bible, as he felt it, had been as a power in his own personal education he had an irresistible desire to communicate to others.

Then Mr. Moody, all through his career as an evangelist, in this country and Great Britain was, though without consciously intending it, an educator of other evangelists, and in fact of the ministry generally. In certain respects of an altogether vital importance he taught them how to preach. He taught them to get off their stilts, to quit their cant, to translate what they learned out of books into the language and modes of thought of the common people.

The Moody Bible Institute of Chicago, the largest school of its kind in the world and the model after which hundreds of others have been formed, was founded in 1886. Speaking of this institution Mr. Moody said, "It seems to me this is the largest thing I have ever undertaken and that it is going to accomplish more than anything I have ever yet been permitted to do." Little did he dream how much that school was going to accomplish!

But Moody was more—he was a philanthropist. He secured millions of dollars for religious and philanthropic enterprises, including the erection of many YMCA buildings and the clearing of the debts from many more.

Mr. Moody could have been an immensely wealthy man had he accepted hymn book royalties which accrued to his personal account to the amount of over $1,500,000. But lest it be said that he preached the gospel for money, he appointed three Christian businessmen as trustees of that fund, and it was by them distributed along various lines of Christian work throughout this country.

Dr. Robert E. Speer came near the mark when he said, "Moody was a combination of General Grant and John B. Gough and Abraham Lincoln and William E. Dodge and Charles Haddon Spurgeon and a few more, but he was not any of them. He was just his own great self, a torrent of love and power, set to sweep men home unto God."

It is to this great servant of God and lover of his fellowmen that we have erected this memorial church. We have two strong reasons for doing so.

First, Chicago is the logical place for Moody's monument. It was here that he began his ministry, and here he learned the secret of reaching men.

Second, this church was the first of all the institutions founded by him.

This building shall ever stand as a testimony to the power of the gospel of God's grace. The ministry of this church for over sixty years is an evidence of the fact that "the gospel is the power of God unto salvation." Week by week, through all these years, the same old story has been told— the story of redeeming love. The grace of Christ has been presented persistently, and scarcely one week has passed in which sinners have not been turned from darkness to light. The Moody Church has never changed its message or its methods since the days of its honored founder.

Sixty-five years ago in a deserted saloon, near what was then known as the Northside Market, this work began. First there was a little Sunday school of barefooted, bare-headed, and dirty urchins in a district noted for bad women and worse men.

In a Sunday school convention held in Canada, Mr. Reynolds of Peoria, Illinois, the secretary of the International Sunday school committee, related the following incident:

> The first time I ever saw him was in a little old shanty that had been abandoned by a saloon keeper. Mr. Moody had got the place to hold a meeting in at night. I went there a little late; and the first thing I saw was a man standing up, with a few tallow candles around him, holding a Negro boy, and trying to read to him the story of the prodigal son; and a great many of the words he could not make out and had to skip. I thought, *if the Lord can ever use such an instrument as that for His honor and glory, it will astonish me.*
>
> After that meeting was over Mr. Moody said to me, "Reynolds, I have got only one talent: I have no education, but I love the Lord Jesus Christ, and I want you to pray for me." I have never ceased from that day to this, morning and night, to pray for that devoted Christian soldier. I have watched him since then, have had counsel with him, and know him thoroughly; and, for consistent walk and conversation, I have never met a man to equal him. It astounds me when I look back and see what Mr. Moody was thirteen years ago, and what he is under God today—shaking Scotland to its very center and reaching now over to Ireland. The last time I heard from him, his injunction was, "Pray for me every day: pray now that God will keep me humble."

The next picture—or glimpse—of Moody is associated with the late Mr. J. V. Farwell, who was Moody's strong friend throughout the years. Mr. Moody applied to this brother for financial help for his work, and after securing the money he asked him if he were engaged in any personal work for Christ. On finding him not fully occupied, he invited him over to his mission Sunday school.

The next Sunday Mr. Farwell appeared as a visitor at the North Market school. The scene was a new one. All his previous Sunday school notions were put to flight. That riotous crowd seemed to be following the example of the Israelites in the time of the Judges, with one essential difference—namely, that each one was doing what was *wrong* in his own eyes, with the evident purpose of mischievous enjoyment. The seats had not yet arrived. The school was leaning up against the walls, and scattered over the floor in every-varying forms, like the figures in the kaleidoscope; jumping, turning somersaults, sparring, whistling, talking out loud, saying "Papers!" "Black your boots!" "Have a shine, mister?"—from which state of confusion they were occasionally rescued by a Scripture reading from Mr. Stillson, or a song from Mr. Trudeau, or a speech from Mr. Moody; only to relapse again into clamor and uproar before the speaker or singer was fairly through.

The emotions of Mr. Farwell, on being introduced to make a speech, were vivid rather than pleasing. He ventured a few words, and only a few, lest he should weary the patience of his audience. But what was his horror, at the close of his remarks, to hear himself nominated by Moody as superintendent of the North Market Mission Sunday school! Before he could object, the school had elected him with a deafening hurrah.

Many honors have fallen to that gentleman since that day; and none of them ever came more unexpectedly, were bestowed more heartily, or brought with them more embarrassment; but he accepted the office to which he was thus suddenly called and entered at once upon its duties, which for more than six years he faithfully continued to perform.

It is a long step from the scene in the old Market Hall to the one here today. Our church now has a membership of 3,436, and 88 of our members are missionaries in foreign lands. Of this number the church supports 67. During the last fiscal year the offerings for foreign missions were more than $36,000—and this in face of the fact that the church has given so sacrificially to the erection of this building.

Again we ask the question, "What mean these stones?" They mean that there is a great Protestant church in the city of Chicago where rich and poor alike are ever welcome and where in spirit and in truth they can worship the God who is the maker of us all. They mean also that this church is to be a base from which heralds of the cross will be sent forth in greater numbers to the ends of the earth to tell the story of redeeming grace. With these larger facilities we feel greater responsibility for sending the gospel to all who have never heard it.

In the years to come, if our Lord tarry, may the story of these stones remain unchanged. May no voice ever be heard in this pulpit that will suggest a question of the inspiration of the Bible or of the authority and authenticity of God's Word. For should such a thing happen, as it has happened in other places, then we may write over this pulpit and over the doors of this church, "Ichabod"—the glory is departed.

When D. L. Moody was a young man he heard the late Henry Varley say, "The world has yet to see what God can do with one who is entirely consecrated to him." And Mr. Moody said in his heart before God, *I will be that man!*

This morning there are before me hundreds of young people. Many of you are looking forward to your life's work. I say to you that I believe God is still looking for men who are entirely consecrated to Him and that He is still waiting to show what He can do through them. "The eyes of the Lord run to and fro throughout the whole earth to show himself strong in the behalf of those whose hearts are perfect toward Him."

As we bow before Him now in prayer I want you to say:

> Take my life and let it be
> Consecrated, Lord, to Thee.

14

Harry Ironside:

Charge That to My Account

A Sermon on Forgiveness

This message on Paul's epistle to Philemon is one of Dr. Ironside's most famous. Cassette tapes of this message, available from Moody Church and other sources, permit today's generation to hear Dr. Ironside's actual delivery.

"If thou count me therefore a partner, receive him as myself. If he hath wronged thee, or oweth thee ought, put that on mine account; I Paul have written it with mine own hand, I will repay it; albeit I do not say to thee how thou owest unto me even thine own self besides" (Philemon 17-19).

Someone has said that this epistle to Philemon is the finest specimen of early private Christian correspondence extant. We should expect this, since it was given by divine inspiration. And yet it all has to do with a thieving runaway slave named Onesimus, who was about to return to his former master.

The history behind the letter, which is deduced from a careful study of the epistle itself, seems to be this: In the city of Colosse dwelt a wealthy Christian man by the name of Philemon, possibly the head of a large household, and like many in that day, he had a number of slaves, or bondsmen. Christianity did not immediately overturn the evil custom of slavery, although eventually it was the means of practically driving it out of the whole civilized world. It began by regulating the relation of master and slave, thus bringing untold blessing to those in bondage.

This man Philemon evidently was converted through the ministry of the apostle Paul. Where they met, we are not told; certainly not in the city of Colosse, because in writing the letter to the Colossians, Paul makes it clear that he had never seen the faces of those who formed the Colossian church. You will recall that he labored at Ephesus for a long period. The fame of his preaching and teaching was spread abroad, and we read that "all in Asia heard the word." Among those who thus heard the gospel message may have been this man Philemon of Colosse, and so he was brought to know Christ.

Some years had gone by, and this slave, Onesimus, had run away. Evidently before going, he had robbed his master. With his ill-gotten gains he had fled to Rome. How he reached there we do not know, but I have no doubt that upon his arrival he had his fling and enjoyed to the full that which had belonged to his master. He did not take God into account, but nevertheless God's eye was upon him when he left his home, and it followed him along the journey from Colosse to Rome. When he reached that great metropolis, he was evidently brought into contact with the very man through whom his master, Philemon, had been converted. Possibly Onesimus was arrested because of some further rascality and in that way came in contact with Paul in prison, or he may have visited him voluntarily. At any rate God, who knows just how to bring the needy sinner and the messenger of the cross together, saw to it that Onesimus and Paul met face to face.

Some years ago there happened a wonderful illustration of this very thing: the divine ability to bring the needy sinner and the messenger of Christ together.

When Sam Hadley [converted drunkard] was in California, just shortly before he died, Dr. J. Wilbur Chapman, that princely man of God, arranged a midnight meeting, using the largest theater in the city of Oakland, in order to get the message of Hadley before the very people who needed it most. On that night a great procession, maybe one thousand people, from all the different churches, led by the Salvation Army band, wended their way through the main streets of the city. Beginning at 10:30, they marched for one-half hour and then came to the Metropolitan Theater. In a moment or two it was packed from floor to gallery.

I happened to be sitting in the first balcony, looking right down upon the stage. I noticed that every seat on the stage was filled with Christian workers, but when Sam Hadley stepped forward to deliver the stirring message of the evening, his seat was left vacant. Just as he began to speak, I saw a man, who had come in at the rear of the stage, slip around from behind the back curtain and stand at one of the wings with his hand up to his ear, listening to the address. Evidently he did not hear very well. In a moment or two he moved to another wing, and then on to another one. Finally he came forward to one side of the front part of the stage and stood there listening, but still he could not hear very well. Upon noticing him, Dr. Chapman immediately got up, greeted the poor fellow, brought him to the front, and put him in the very chair which Sam Hadley had occupied. There he listened entranced to the story of Hadley's redemption.

When the speaker had finished, Dr. Chapman arose to close the meeting, and Hadley took Chapman's chair next to this man. Turning to the man he shook hands with him, and they chatted together. When Dr. Chapman was about ready to ask the people to rise and receive the benediction, Hadley suddenly sprang to his feet, and said, "Just a moment, my friends. Before we close, Dr. Chapman, may I say something? When I was on my way from New York to Oakland a couple of weeks ago, I stopped at Detroit. I was traveling in a private car, put at my disposal by a generous Christian manufacturer. While my car was in the yards, I went downtown and addressed a group at a mission. As I finished, an old couple came up and said, 'Mr. Hadley, won't you go home and take supper with us?'

"I replied, 'You must excuse me; I am not at all well, and it is a great strain for me to go out and visit between meetings. I had better go back to the car and rest.'

"They were so disappointed. The mother faltered. 'Oh, Mr. Hadley, we did want to see you so badly about something.'

"Very well, give me a few moments to lie down, and I will go with you."

He then told how they sat together in the old-fashioned parlor, on the horse-hair furniture, and talked. They told him their story; "Mr. Hadley, you know we have a son, Jim. Our son was brought up to go to Sunday school and church, and oh, we had such hopes of him. But he had to work out rather early in life, and he got into association with worldly men and went down and down and down. By and by he came under the power of strong drink. We shall never forget the first time he came home drunk. Sometimes he would never get home at all until the early hours of the morning. Our hearts were breaking over him. One time he did not come all night, but early in the morning, after we had waited through a sleepless night for him. He came in hurriedly, with a pale face, and said, 'Folks, I cannot stay; I must get out. I did something when I was drunk last night, and if it is found out, it will go hard with me. I am not going to stay here and blot your name.' He kissed us both and left, and until recently we have never seen nor heard of him.

"Mr Hadley, here is a letter that just came from a friend who lives in California, and he tells us, 'I am quite certain that I saw your son, Jim, in San Francisco. I was coming down on a street car and saw him waiting for a car. I was carried by a block. I hurried back, but he had boarded another car and was gone. I know it was Jim.'

"He is still living, Mr. Hadley, and we are praying that God will save him yet. You are going to California to have meetings out there. Daily we will be kneeling here praying that God will send our boy, Jim, to hear you, and perhaps when he learns how God saved one poor drunkard, he will know there is hope also for him. Will you join us in daily prayer?"

Hadley said he would, and they prayed together. "They made me promise that every day at a given hour, Detroit time, I would lift my heart to God in fellowship with them, knowing that they were kneeling in that room, praying God that He would reach Jim and give me the opportunity of bringing him to Christ. That was two weeks ago. I have kept my promise every day. My friends, this is my first meeting in California, and here is Jim. Tonight he was drinking in a saloon on Broadway as the great procession passed. He heard the singing, followed us to the theater, and said, 'I believe I will go in.' He hurried up here, but it was too late. Every place was filled, and the police officer said, 'We cannot allow another person to go inside.' Jim thought, 'This is just my luck. Even if I want to go and hear the gospel, I cannot. I will go back to the saloon.' He started back; then he returned determined to see if there was not some way to get in. He came in the back door and finally sat in my own chair. Friends, Jim wants Christ, and I ask you all to pray for him."

There that night we saw that poor fellow drop on his knees and confess his sin and guilt and accept Christ as his Savior. The last sight we had of Jim was when J. Wilbur Chapman and he were on their way to the Western Union Telegraph office to send the joyful message: "God heard your prayers. My soul is saved." Oh, what a God, lover of sinners that He is! He delights to reach the lost and needy!

This same God was watching over Onesimus. He saw him when he stole that money and as he fled from his master's house. He watched him on his way to Rome and in due time brought him face to face with Paul. Through that same precious gospel that had been blest to the salvation of Philemon, Onesimus, the thieving runaway slave, was also saved, and another star was addded to the Redeemer's crown.

Then I can imagine Onesimus coming to Paul and saying, "Now, Paul, I want your advice. There is a matter which is troubling me. You know my master, Philemon. I must confess that I robbed him and ran away. I feel now that I must go back and try to make things right."

One evidence that people are really born of God is their effort to make restitution for wrong done in the past. They want a good conscience both before God and man.

"Paul, ought I to go back in accordance with the Roman law? I have nothing to pay, and I don't know just what to do. I do not belong to myself, and it is quite impossible to ever earn anything to make up for the loss. Will you advise me what to do?"

Paul might have said, "I know Philemon well. He has a tender, kind, loving heart and a forgiving spirit. I will write him a note and ask him to forgive you, and that will make everything all right."

But he did not do that. Why? I think that he wanted to give us a wonderful picture of the great gospel of vicarious substitution. One of the primary aspects of the work of the cross is substitution. The Lord Jesus Christ Himself paid the debt that we owe to the infinite God, in order that when forgiveness came to us it would be on a perfectly righteous basis. Paul, who had himself been justified through the cross, now says, "I will write a letter to Philemon and undertake to become your surety. You go back to Philemon and present my letter. You do not need to plead your own case; just give him my letter."

We see Onesimus with that message from Paul safely hidden in his wallet, hurrying back to Colosse. Imagine Philemon standing on the portico of his beautiful residence, looking down the road, and suddenly exclaiming, "Why, who is that? It certainly looks like that scoundrel, Onesimus! But surely he would not have the face to come back. Still, it looks very much like him. I will just watch and wait."

A little later, he says, "I declare, it *is* Onesimus! He seems to be coming to the house. I suppose he has had a hard time in the world. The stolen money is all gone, and now perhaps he is coming to beg for pardon."

As he comes up the pathway, Onesimus calls, "Master, Master!"

"Well, Onesimus, are you home again?"

"Yes, Master, read this, please."

No other word would Onesimus speak for himself; Paul's letter would explain all.

Philemon takes the letter, opens it, and begins to read: *Paul, a prisoner of Jesus Christ.*

"Why, Onesimus, where did you meet Paul? Did you see him personally?"

"Yes, Master, in the prison in Rome; he led me to Christ."

Unto Philemon our dearly beloved, and fellowlabourer.

"Little enough I have ever done, but that is just like Paul."

And to our beloved Apphia (That was Mrs. Philemon.)

"Come here, Apphia. Here is a letter from Paul."

When Mrs. Philemon sees Onesimus, she exclaims, "Are you back?"

One can imagine her mingled disgust and indignation as she sees him standing there. But Philemon says: "Yes, my dear, not a word. Here is a letter for us to read—a letter from Paul."

Running on down the letter he comes to this: *Yet for love's sake I rather beseech thee, being such an one as Paul the aged, and now also a prisoner of Jesus Christ. I beseech thee for my son Onesimus.*

"Think of that! He must have been putting it over on Paul in some way or another."

Whom I have begotten in my bonds. "I wonder if he told him anything about the money he stole from us. I suppose he has been playing the religious game with Paul."

Which in time past was to thee unprofitable.

"I am not so sure of that."

Whom I have sent again.

"Paul must have thought a lot of him. If he didn't serve him any better than he did me, he would not get much out of him." He goes on reading through the letter.

"Well, well, that rascally, thieving liar! Maybe Paul believes that he is saved, but I will never believe it unless I find out that he owned up to the wrong he did me."

What is this? *If he hath wronged thee, or oweth thee ought, put that on my account; I Paul have written it with mine own hand, I will repay it: albeit I do not say to thee how thou owest unto me even thine own self besides.*

Oh, I think in a moment Philemon was conquered. "Why," he says, "it is all out then. He has confessed his sin. He has acknowledged his thieving, owned his guilt, and, just think, Paul, that dear servant of God, suffering in prison for Christ's sake, says: *Put that on my account. I will settle everything for him.* Paul becomes his surety." It was just as though Paul should write today: "Charge that to my account!"

Is not this a picture of the gospel? A picture of what the Savior has done for every repentant soul? I think I see Him as he brings the needy, penitent sinner into the presence of God and says, "My Father, he has wronged Thee, he owes Thee much, but all has been charged to My account. Let him go free." How could the Father turn aside the prayer of His Son after that death of shame and sorrow on Calvary's cross, when He took our blame upon Himself and suffered in our stead?

But now observe it is not only that Paul offered to become Onesimus's surety, it was not merely that he offered to settle everything for Onesimus in regard to the past, but he provided for his future too. He says to Philemon: *"If thou count me therefore a partner, receive him as myself."*

Is not that another aspect of our salvation? We are "accepted in the beloved." The blessed Savior brings the redeemed one into the presence of the Father and says, "My Father, if thou countest Me the partner of Thy throne, receive him as Myself." Paul says, *"Not now as a servant, but above a servant, a brother beloved, specially to me, but how much more unto thee, both in the flesh, and in the Lord?"* He is to take the place not of a bondsman but of an honored member of the family and a brother in Christ. Think of it— once a poor, thieving, runaway slave, and now a recognized servant of Christ, made welcome for Paul's sake. Thus our Father saves the lawless, guilty sinner, and makes him welcome for Jesus' sake, treating him as He treats His own beloved.

Jesus paid it all,
All to Him I owe;
Sin had left a crimson stain:
He washed it white as snow.

And now every redeemed one is "in Christ before God—yea, made the righteousness of God in him." Oh, wondrous love! Justice is satisfied. What a picture we have here then of substitution and acceptance. The apostle Paul epitomized it all for us: "Who was delivered for our offences, and was raised again for our justification" (Romans 4:25).

We are accepted in the Beloved. The Lord Jesus became our Surety, settled for all our past, and has provided for all our future. In the book of Proverbs (11:15) there is a very striking statement, "He that is surety for a stranger shall smart for it; and he that hateth suretyship is sure." These words were written, centuries before the cross, to warn men of what is still a very common ground for failure and ruin in business life. To go surety for a stranger is a very dangerous thing, as thousands have learned to their sorrow. It is poor policy to take such a risk unless you are prepared to lose.

But there was One who knew to the full what all the consequences of His act would be, and yet, in grace, deigned to become "surety for a stranger." Meditate upon these wonderful words: "For ye know the grace of our Lord Jesus Christ, that, though he was rich, yet for your sakes he became poor, that ye through his poverty might be rich" (2 Corinthians 8:9). He was the stranger's Surety.

A surety is one who stands good for another. Many a man will do this for a friend, long known and trusted; but no wise man will so act for a stranger, unless he is prepared to lose. But it was when we were strangers and foreigners and enemies and alienated in our minds by wicked works, that Jesus in grace became our Surety. "Christ also hath once suffered for sins, the just for the unjust, that he might bring us to God."

All we owed was exacted from Him when He suffered upon the tree for sins not His own. He could then say, "I restored that which I took not away (Psalm 69:4). Bishop Lowth's beautiful rendering of Isaiah 53:7 reads: "It was exacted and He became answerable." This is the very essence of the gospel message. He died in my place; He paid my debt.

How fully He proved the truth of the words quoted from Proverbs, when He suffered on that cross of shame! How He had to "smart for it" when God's awful judgment against sin fell upon Him. But He wavered not! In love to God and to the strangers whose Surety He had become, "He endured the cross, despising the shame."

His sorrows are now forever past. He has paid the debt, met every claim in perfect righteousness. The believing sinner is cleared of every charge, and God is fully glorified.

He bore on the tree
The sentence for me,
And now both the Surety
And sinner are free.

None other could have met the claims of God's holiness against the sinner and have come out triumphant at last. He alone could atone for sin. Because He has settled every claim, God has raised Him from the dead and seated Him at His own right hand in highest glory.

Have you trusted "the stranger's Surety"? If not, turn to Him now while grace is free.

15

Alan Redpath:

God Has a Plan for Your Life

A Christian Life Sermon

*B*lessed *be the Lord who daily loadeth us with benefits, the God of our salvation.*
(Psalm 68:19)

The most wonderful thing about life is to know that God has a purpose for every one of His children, and it is identical, whoever they may be. He also had a plan for each of us as individuals which is absolutely different in every life. His purpose is to make us like Himself and concerns what we are to become. His plan is related to His purpose and is concerned with what we do.

This particular verse from the Psalms is interesting because of the variety of ways in which it is translated. The Revised Standard Version says, "Blessed be the Lord, who daily bears us up. God is our salvation." The *New International Version* renders it, "The Lord bears our burdens." The [King James] is quoted as our text. So one might say these are somewhat contradictory, but perhaps we should look at them as two sides of the same coin. He only really bears our burdens as we are prepared to accept the load He places on us.

The trouble in the world today is demonstrated by a clash of wills: nation against nation; person against person. The believer will know a desperate clash of wills in submitting to the purpose of God for his life. Our freedom of choice is part of God's will. When Jesus chose His disciples, He chose them so that first of all they were to be with Him (Mark 3:14). Fellowship with Him is His desire, but it cannot be forced. Freedom to continue or to break it off is left to us. We can have as much of God as we want—no more and no less.

His purpose for each person is always the same, but His will and plan for an individual may change. His purpose for our character is permanently revealed in Christ, to conform us to His likeness (Romans 8:29), but His will for our career has to be sought by each of us as we obey Romans 12:1-2. But He never reveals His will until we accept His purpose for us without necessarily knowing what it will be.

Now to look at our verse. The Greek word in the Old Testament Septuagint version is rendered "*loading*," but in the New Testament is translated "bearing." That is, there are things we are to carry for Christ, and as we consider some of these things, we shall see His plan revealed to us so that His purpose may be fulfilled in us.

1. *His shoes*

"He that comes after me is mightier than I, whose shoes I am not worthy to bear" (Matthew 3:11). The Christian life starts when we become bond-slaves to the Lord Jesus, when we are ready for anything, however lowly. This is not an advanced or mature Christian experience, but only the beginning of it. Never underestimate the ability of human beings to get themselves thoroughly tangled up with Scripture truths until it ceases to be truth and becomes downright falsehood. There is a real danger of preaching a divided Christ: that we may accept Him as Savior without yielding to Him as Lord.

The only object of saving faith is Christ Himself, not His saviorhood or His lordship, but Christ Himself. God does not offer salvation to someone who will believe on one of His attributes but reject others. It is quite impossible for anyone to come to Christ for His help and yet have no intention of obeying Him. Christ's saviorhood is forever united wit His lordship (Romans 10:9–13). Note that in Scripture He is invariably referred to as "*our Lord and Savior.*"

We must learn that it is not until we take our place as servant that He will take His place as Lord. Christ must be Lord, or He will not be Savior. But that is not to say that the earnest Christian may not go on to explore ever-increasing blessings in Christ, nor is it suggested that our first saving contact with Him brings perfect knowledge of all that He is. All to the contrary, for life is not long enough to allow us to experience all the riches of His grace. As we discover more and more of Him, and make that discovery ours, we grow in the knowledge of our Lord, and His sovereignty is extended over ever increasing areas of our lives.

But life begins in submission to His lordship, for the Holy Spirit is given to them who obey Him (Acts 5:32). As this relationship becomes mature, we become more and more conscious of what sin is. The Lord puts His finger on things in our lives and says, "This is not My will for you, and it has to go." When Jesus has you for anything, you have Him for everything.

2. *His name*

Paul was to be "a chosen instrument to bear my name" (Acts 9:15). To bear the name of another person is to act as his representative or, in the diplomatic sense, to be an ambassador (2 Corinthians 5:20). As followers of the Lord Jesus we are called to bear His name faithfully (not necessarily successfully), to represent Him to others without marring His character, and to be guardian of His reputation. This demands a careful walk with Him, as Paul commands in Ephesians 5:5-17. The days are evil, and it is imperative that those of us who name the name of Christ should live worthy of our high calling, and in bearing His name, not besmirch His reputation or lower His standards.

Some years ago a well-known evangelist was visiting an East Anglican town and staying with a Christian couple who had in their home a German au pair girl who called herself an atheist. Before the guest arrived, the hostess told the girl he was to receive every courtesy and then asked her to get the meat for the Sunday dinner. The details were very specific, and when the German girl gave them to the butcher he said, "You must be having someone important staying with you!"

"Not really," replied the girl, "but with the fuss they are making you would think it was the good Lord Himself, not just a preacher!" And she stormed out of the shop.

The next week she returned for a further order, and the butcher said to her, "Well, how are you getting on with your preacher friend?"

The girl hesitated, then said, "You remember I said you would think the good Lord was coming to our house? Well, He came!"

3. *His cross*

"Whoever does not bear his own cross, and come after me, cannot be my disciple" (Luke 14:27).

What do you understand by the cross in this connotation?

What strange ideas people have about the cross! A man spoke to me after a service and said he had an awful temper. "That must be my cross," he added. I said to him, "That is not your cross; it is your wife's cross, but your sin!"

The cross is something you bear with Jesus and share with Him—His shame, His persecution, His loneliness. Read Corinthians 9:4-12 to see what Paul bore for Christ's sake. He was entitled to normal rations (v. 4), to normal romance (v. 5), to normal recreation (v. 6), to normal remuneration (v. 7-11). But the Lord was dearer than all (v. 12), and he was willing to put them all aside in order to be identified with Jesus in His death to self.

4. *His marks*

"I bear in my body the marks of the Lord Jesus" (Galations 6:17). The word "marks" speaks of the branding of a slave, "stigmata." What marks was Paul speaking about? He tells of the thorn in the flesh he endured (2 Corinthians 12:7), which may have been blindness at his conversion from which he never fully recovered (see Galatians 4:15).

Whatever, he was rejoicing in them, not moaning about them. Do you and I have any marks that would betray us as His followers? We do not bear His marks by negative living but by positive identity with the life of the Lord Jesus lived in and through us by the Holy Spirit.

Some years ago at a Keswick-type convention in Chicago, a dear friend from England gave me a piece of paper bearing a poem by Amy Carmichael. I did not think too much about it, though I thanked him for it and quickly read it. I have found it again recently and wondered, "Was this meant for me at that time?" I think it was. Here is the poem:

> Has thou no scar?
> No hidden scar on foot, or side or hand?
> I hear thee sung as mighty in the land.
> I hear them hail thy bright ascendant star:
> Has thou no scar?
> No wound? No scar?
> Yet as the Master shall the servant be,
> And pierced are the feet that follow Me;
> But thine are whole: can he have followed far
> Who has nor wound nor scar?

You may not talk about the marks you know that God has put upon you, but as the years go by you know that growth is costly because it involves the marks of the cross—only then will the Holy Spirit be released.

There is one final thing we must bear:

5. *His image*

"As we have borne the image of the earthly, so shall we bear the image of the heavenly" (1 Corinthians 15:49).

What a prospect! An advertisement for a life insurance company read, "Compare our life plan with others, and see if we do not give greater benefits than any!" What about God's plan? How unique it is, for He daily loads us with benefits. But in order to bear the image of the heavenly one day, I must have the Lord Jesus in all His power and glory now, for flesh and blood cannot inherit the kingdom of God.

What about you? Are you bearing your share of the load? Are you His slave bearing His shoes?

Do you bear His name as His ambassador?

Do you bear His cross as His fellow sufferer? Do you bear His marks as His partner?

Only then can we really pray and experience revival in our own lives, in our churches, in our land.

If you do, one day you will bear His image! May there not be such a great difference on that day when we meet Him, because as we have walked in His plan, we have been made wonderfully like Him.

Prayer

Father, give me grace to fulfill Your conditions so that Your purpose may be revealed in and through me.

You were a servant: make me one too. Show me what You would have me do. To make me a servant, make me like You.

16

George Sweeting:

Holding the Ropes

A Sermon of Encouragement

*A*nd *after that many days were fulfilled, the Jews took counsel to kill him: But their laying await was known of Saul. And they watched the gates day and night to kill him.*

Then the disciples took him by night and let him down by the wall in a basket. (Acts 9:23–25)

How did Saul get into this predicament? Only a short time before he had been Saul, brilliant, extremely religious, and ruthless in his attempt to rid the world of the followers of Jesus. He was convinced that Jesus was an imposter and His followers were heretics, and because he felt chosen to dispose of this threat to the Jewish belief in the unity of God, he zealously worked to capture and jail or even kill any Christians he could find.

But God Himself captured Saul. He caught him as Saul was going to Damascus to hunt Christians, and Saul went to Damascus a changed man. In fact, he "preached Christ in the synagogues, that He is the Son of God" (Acts 9:20). The people were amazed; some were skeptical; some were as intolerant of Saul as he had been of them.

Consequently Saul began to receive the treatment he had been giving out. He became a hunted man. It was no longer safe for him to walk the streets of Damascus, for soldiers were everywhere. What was he to do? Fortunately, Saul had friends, believers in Christ, who cared for him. They led him stealthily through the shadows of the city to the Damascus wall. Then, hidden in a large basket, Saul was lowered through a window. The disciples slowly played out the ropes that held the basket until they heard it thud to the ground, then heard Saul crawl quietly out and move away into the darkness.

We know what happened to Saul after his escape from Damascus, but what became of the disciples who held the ropes? Who were they? Where did they go? What did they do? Why were they willing to risk their lives for someone they may have barely known?

Nobody knows. Nothing more is said about them. Their names are never mentioned. They remain unknown to history, unknown to us. But God knows them. And that is enough. Those disciples were truly servants, for they served without recognition.

Too often people will serve as long as they get publicity. They will donate food or clothing to the poor, starving people—if their names are printed in the church bulletin. They will give money to build buildings—if a plaque on the wall will carry their names.

Jesus said, "Beware of doing your good deeds conspicuously to catch men's eyes or you will miss the reward of your heavenly Father" (Matthew 6:1). In fact, He suggested such secrecy that the left hand would not know what the right hand did.

Whether or not the rope holders knew this injunction, they weren't concerned. They did the job that was required of them, then disappeared. How many Christians do you know who serve in this way? There must be scores of doctors, mechanics, lawyers, janitors, salesclerks, teachers, secretaries, garbage collectors, executives, homemakers, who go about their business from day to day, serving Christ in their own way, doing what is required of them.

They hold the ropes, perhaps performing services that don't seem particularly Christian—on the surface, anyway. These people follow in a tradition of rope holders who steadfastly served without publicity.

Perhaps the greatest unknown servants are parents. Today we read a lot about the generation gap, about teenagers rebelling against their parents. This is the way it has been throughout history; it is human nature to resist restraint.

Yet many of us are followers of Christ because of our parents. They patiently suffered through our growing up. They loved us in spite of ourselves and continued to love until we were ready to be on our own—until our basket touched the ground.

When did the disciples hold the ropes? It was night. The escape had to be made at night since daylight was as dangerous for the disciples as it was for Saul. But they weren't really safe at night either. For their fight was "against the unseen power that controls this dark world, and spiritual agents for the very headquarters of evil" (Ephesians 6:12). So is ours. It seems to me it's fairly easy to be a Christian in the daylight, when we can see where we're going and when life is uncomplicated. But what happens when darkness falls? What do we do when we're not sure which direction to take because the paths are confused? How do we react when life seems to have no point? Is that the time to forget Christ?

Some do. Peter did—for a time, at least. He was right there holding the ropes when Jesus was popular. But when trouble came, Peter denied his Lord. And Peter had been convinced that he would never do such a thing! We probably all feel like Peter at times.

Though most of us have not been in such a crucial position, some Christians are in constant danger. I know of a minister in East Germany who met with a group of young American Christians. The visiting teenagers were dumbfounded when he carefully shut all the windows in his apartment even though the day was stifling. He explained that he was afraid of being overheard in a discussion of Christianity. Though this pastor could have escaped East Germany, he chose to stay with his underground church. He is holding the ropes for his flock, who worship Jesus Christ in fear for their lives. In some countries, our age is not so different from Saul's.

This is an age of opportunity, an age of excitement—but at the same time, an age of terror. We have sent men into space, and we have discovered ways of prolonging life. Yet we still do not understand our own world, and we still manufacture implements of war. We produce food that rots in stockpiles while millions of people in our own country and abroad slowly starve to death. We send missionaries to Africa and India and South America—but our neighbors in Skokie and South Holland and Lawndale do not hear words of love from us. It is a dark age masquerading as an age of enlightenment. Where will it end? What can you do?

Hold the ropes, my friends. Hang on tight. Don't let go. God has chosen you; the missionaries you pray for count on you; your children count on you; your neighbors need you; your church needs you. Keep holding the ropes in spite of the confusion surrounding us. Saul's friends did not give up.

How long did the disciples hold the ropes? They held until the basket touched the ground. They didn't drop it halfway because it got heavy or they got tired. Saul trusted them to hang on until he was on the ground.

Someone has said that "the greatest ability is dependability." It did't take any great ability for the disciples to hold the ropes. They just had to hang on until they were sure Saul was safe.

That's the key. Once you put yourself in a position of becoming a rope holder, you can't give up. You can't be responsible for everybody, that's true. You'd be exhausted. But you are responsible for certain people.

For some, you may be the only one holding the ropes. What about the widow living next door to you? Her children all live out of town; she hasn't many friends. Who is there to care about her? Perhaps you're the only one.

Then there are those high school boys who hang around with your son. Where are their parents? Why are the kids always at your house? Maybe they need an adult friend to care about them.

And how about those men you have lunch with every day—those busy executives? Do they know anybody else who can show them the love of Christ, or is it up to you?

Of course, trying to be a rope holder may be discouraging. You may serve the widow countless dinners and numberless cups of coffee and still have little chance to talk to her about Christ. Just when you think the kids really accept you, they may back away. And your business acquaintances may never want to consider what Christ has to say to them. All your praying, all your active showing of love may seem useless.

But are you looking for a reward? Or are you trying to serve Christ? Perhaps you won't see results as you serve. Then again, you might. You never know what God is going to do. You never know when your prayer will be answered or how it will be answered.

So keep praying, keep asking, keep seeking, keep knocking—until your basket reaches the ground, until the answer is found. Then you can let go of the ropes.

Why did the disciples hold the ropes? Perhaps their reason was simple—someone was in trouble, and they could help. Those men didn't really know who they were helping to escape. Oh, they knew something about Saul. They knew what he had been and what he had become. But that was all.

They had no idea he would preach in some of the most important places in their world—Jerusalem, Antioch, Cyprus. They didn't imagine that he would start churches all over Asia, including Corinth and Rome. They did not dream he would write letters that would become part of the Scripture. To them he was Saul, a believer, and their friend. They were not concerned with who he might be or what he might become. They were concerned about doing their job faithfully.

You may not know who's in your basket. When she hid him in a basket, did Moses' mother know her son would deliver his people from slavery? Did D. L. Moody's mother know what he would become? Did the people who helped Jews escape Germany during World War II know what their charges would become? Do you suppose Sirhan Sirhan's role in history might have been different if someone had been holding the ropes for him?

None of us really knows about the people we carry in our baskets. But we all have someone. And we must be faithful—as Christ is faithful to us. God doesn't give us a bigger task than we can handle. But He expects us to do the job assigned to us. David did his job—with a slingshot. Gideon did his—with a jar. An unknown woman did hers—with a vial of oil.

Are we doing our job? Are we holding the ropes for the people God has given us? Will we hang on until their baskets safely touch ground?

Christ has called us to be servants. He has called us to be holders. Let us follow Him.

17

Warren Wiersbe:

Start Your Week with a Miracle

A Church Life Sermon

Text: Hebrews 10:19-25

There was a time when you would wake up on Sunday morning and immediately know that it was Sunday. There was a different atmosphere. Certain sounds were missing, and a spirit of worship was in the air. But I fear that that time is long gone. Sunday, at least in the city, is getting just like any other day. You hear the whirl of power mowers and the roar of automobiles; and when you go to church, you pass shopping centers that are jammed with cars. The spirit of the world has invaded the Lord's Day, and I fear that this spirit has invaded our Christian homes, our hearts, and our churches. Without realizing it, we have allowed this spirit of worldliness to erode our spirituality.

It is this situation that prompts me to talk with you on the subject "Start Your Week with a Miracle." The way you begin something pretty much determines how things will turn out. God has established the Lord's Day as a day of worship for us who are God's people. We can worship on any day, and we don't judge one another as to our manner of worship. But God has established the Lord's Day especially as a day of worship for God's people. I realize that some people, because of physical handicap or employment, cannot be in the house of the Lord every Lord's Day. But if you and I will start each week with a miracle—the miracle of worship—it will make a difference in our lives. This miracle is described in Hebrews 10:19-25:

Having therefore, brethren, boldness to enter into the holiest by the blood
of Jesus, by a new and living way, which he hath consecrated for us, through
the veil, that is to say, his flesh; and having an high priest over the house of
God; let us draw near with a true heart in full assurance of faith, having our
hearts sprinkled from an evil conscience, and our bodies washed with pure
water. Let us hold fast the profession of our faith without wavering; (for he is
faithful that promised;) and let us consider one another to provoke unto love
and to good works: not forsaking the assembling of ourselves together, as the
manner of some is; but exhorting one another: and so much the more, as ye
see the day approaching.

I want to focus on the statement "Not forsaking the assembling of
ourselves together." The next time you are tempted to neglect or abandon
the public worship of God, please consider what you are doing. In fact,
from this passage there are four considerations that compel us to be faithful
in our public worship of God.

First of all, *consider the Lord Jesus Christ.* Consider what He did for you
that you might have the privilege of assembling with God's people and
worshiping God. He died for you. Verse 19 mentions "the blood of Jesus."
The public worship of God, when the saints of God come together, is a
costly thing. For us to come into the very presence of God meant that Jesus
Christ had to die on the cross. He took upon Himself a human body, and
His body was rent, as it were, on the cross. When His body was rent, the
veil was rent. Now there is an open way into the presence of God, an open
way that cost Him His life. He died and arose again that He might open for
us "the new and living way."

When you and I neglect, ignore, or abandon the public worship of God,
we are insulting the Lord Jesus Christ. The Lord's Day is the *Lord's* day. It's
not our day. We must consider Him first of all.

Consider the Lord Jesus Christ, not only what He *did* for you but what
He is *now* doing for you. The theme of the book of Hebrews is our Lord's
present ministry for us in heaven. He is our high priest in heaven, praying
for us. He is interceding for us at the throne of grace. The Lord Jesus Christ
is working for us and in us, seeking to perfect us. Hebrews 13:20, "Now the
God of peace, that brought again from the dead our Lord Jesus, that great
shepherd of the sheep, through the blood of the everlasting covenant, make
you perfect in every good work to do his will, working in you that which
is wellpleasing in his sight, through Jesus Christ; to whom be glory for ever
and ever. Amen." In heaven, the Lord Jesus Christ is at work perfecting
you and praying for you. Now the least we can do is to assemble together
with God's people to praise Him, to worship Him, and to do the thing He
has commanded us to do.

The writer tells us that we should consider Christ because of what He
has done for us and because of what He is now doing for us. But we should

also consider what He *shall do* for us. At the end of verse 25 he says, "You see the day approaching." What day? The day when Jesus Christ shall come and take us to heaven. Worship on earth is a foretaste of heaven above. If you and I are bored with worship on earth, what are we going to do when we enter into the very presence of God to worship and adore Him forever?

The next time you are tempted to neglect or abandon the public worship of God, consider Jesus Christ. Consider what He did for you, what He is doing for you, and what He shall do for you.

There is a second consideration here in Hebrews 10. In verses 22-23 he exhorts us to *consider ourselves*. He is not asking us to be selfish but to remember that we need each other. "Let us draw near.... Let us hold fast the profession of our faith." We need one another. We need the Body. We are sheep in the fold. We are stones in the temple. We are soldiers in the army. We are children in the family. We need the public worship of God.

Let's talk about your personal Christian life. Is there a *deadness* to your Christian life? Well, then you need to come by this "living way." Is there a dullness in your life? Public worship takes us on this "new ... way" that leads us out of dullness. When I find a Christian who ignores the public worship of God, that Christian is dead and dull. He is ignoring "the new and living way."

There is also the problem of *distance*. "Let us draw near." Do you ever feel that you are far from God? Are there times when you feel that God is far from you? We know He isn't far from us, because God never leaves us or forsakes us. But sometimes it feels like He is far from us and we are far from Him. The writer says in effect, "Start worshiping God! Draw near to God!" "Draw nigh unto God and He will draw nigh unto you," is what James tells us. How do we draw high to God? By confessing our sins, by praising Him, by thanking Him, by listening to His Word—and these things add up to *worship!*

What a delightful experience it is to draw near to God! I've had times in my own Christian life when things have been dead, dull, and distant. Then I've gone to church, and God has moved in to give me a new touch. I think all of us need that regularly.

There is also the problem of *doubt*. "Let us draw near with a true heart in full assurance of faith." Christians have doubts. There is a difference between doubt and unbelief. The book of Hebrews warns us against "an evil heart of unbelief," because unbelief is an act of the will. We say, "I *will not* believe what God says!" But doubt is a problem of the mind and the heart. We wonder whether God will answer prayer, meet our needs, or show us His will. The writer says, "Why don't you draw near with a true heart in full assurance of faith, and your doubts will be taken care of." You go to the house of God, you praise and you worship Him, and He strengthens your faith. You listen to His Word, you fellowship with God's people, and your doubts start to disappear. "Faith comes by hearing and hearing by the Word of God."

There is always the problem of *defilement*. Even though we seek to walk with the Lord and obey Him, just by living in this world, we get defiled. The mind gets defiled, the heart gets defiled. All around us is an atmosphere that is defiling. The writer says, "Let's have our hearts sprinkled from an evil conscience, and our bodies washed with pure water." He is comparing our worship with that of the Hebrew priests. They had to go through certain ceremonies before they could serve God in the Tabernacle and Temple. We come to the Lord Jesus Christ in worship, He cleanses us, and He fills us. The conscience is made pure, the heart is cleansed.

There may be a problem of *discouragement*. "Let us hold fast the profession of our faith without wavering." Some translations read, "The profession of our *hope* without wavering." Faith and hope go together, and they conquer discouragement. Worship is what prepared you for life. You worship every day, I know, in your own private home; but we ought to be assembled together as the people of God. The Christian who considers himself will see how important worship really is.

Third, the next time you are tempted to neglect and abandon the public worship of God, *consider other Christians*. Verse 24 says, "Let us consider one another." "One another" is a key phrase in the New Testament. "Love one another." "Pray for one another." "Edify one another." "Care for one another." Encourage one another." "Wash one another's feet." "Let us provoke one another." We are not to provoke one another in the sense of making people angry. It means "stimulating one another"—encouraging one another—to love and good works. By being in the house of God, you encourage your pastor, the minister of music, the choir, and you are encouraging other Christians in their worship. If I am missing, I make it easier for somebody else to disobey God. They say, "Well, Wiersbe wasn't there, so why should *I* be there?" If we consider each other, we will provoke each other to love and encourage each other to meet together to worship and serve Christ.

When we encourage one another "to love and good works," we build a better church, and this makes for better homes and better communities. Are you provoking others to love God? By your faithful worship, are you provoking others to worship God and to love one another? Are you encouraging people to do good works and to serve the Lord, or are they using you as an excuse for doing nothing?

Let's consider Christ, let's consider ourselves, let's consider one another; and finally, *let's consider the lost*. The public worship of God is a witness to the unsaved world. When your neighbors see you walking out on Sundays carrying your Bible, they say, "Oh, yes, they are going to church. Why are they going to church?'' *Because Jesus is alive!* When you go to church on the Lord's Day, you are bearing witness of the resurrection of the Lord Jesus Christ. You are saying, "He's alive!" You don't go week by week to worship a dead person. Others know you are going to worship Jesus Christ. The public worship of God is a united witness of the church to the whole world that Jesus Christ is alive, because the Lord's Day is the day of resurrection.

We are also witnessing to others that heaven is real, that the spiritual is real, that there is more to this life than eating and drinking, buying and selling, the routine things that go on during the week. There is nothing wrong with these things, but if you leave God out, "what shall it profit a man if he gains the whole world and loses his own soul?"

We are bearing witness that Jesus is alive, that heaven is real, that salvation is real, and that Jesus is coming again. "As we see the day approaching. . . .''

You see, the worship of the Lord Jesus Christ on the first day of the week is not a luxury; it is a necessity. *We need it.* Worship is not only a responsibility; it is a privilege. We start the week with a miracle. We begin each week in the presence of God, in public worhip, and we consider Jesus Christ, our living Savior. We consider what He did for us, what He is doing for us, and what He shall do for us when He returns. We are also considering ourselves. We are helping to build ourselves up spiritually. The inner man must be fed the truth of God's Word just as the outer man has to be fed food. The inner man also needs cleansing, "clothing," and strengthening. The greatest thing you can do for yourself is to share in the public worship of God.

Start your week with a miracle. It will lead to a week of miracles as you worship Christ and walk with Him!

18

Erwin Lutzer:

The Renewing of the Mind

A Sermon for Daily Living

On Sunday, April 3, 1977, Erwin Lutzer preached in the pulpit of Moody Church for the first time, when Warren Wiersbe suddenly became ill. This is the sermon Lutzer delivered. It later appeared in Moody Monthly *magazine under the title "Those Sins That Won't Budge."*

You give your anxiety to God, but an hour later its weight is back on your shoulders.

You ask God to control your temper, but you blow your top.

You pray that you will not lust and even reckon yourself to be dead to sinful impulses. But the next day you can't push that tall blonde out of your mind.

Every Christian at one time or another yields to God, only to be squeezed back into the same mold, the same habits.

Can we really be delivered from the one-step-forward and two-steps-back routine? At times I've thought the answer was no. Despite my sincere attempts at yielding myself to God, I retained certain weaknesses (*sins* is a more honest word) that I concluded I would simply have to live with. "We're all human, you know!"

But I knew my private failure was no credit to the Christ who won the victory on the cross. Did He not promise that we could be *free indeed?* That might not mean perfection, but surely it implies spiritual progress—moral and spiritual liberation.

About a year ago I heard a sermon that helped dislodge me from my spiritual roller coaster. Biblical principles were presented that convinced me that I need not compromise with sin, even those secret ones that were safely tucked away in the inner crevices of my soul.

The remedy was not surrender to God; I had already done that as fully as I knew how. Nor was it a further explanation of how to reckon myself to be dead to sin; I had already rejoiced in my union with Christ. Such matters are necessary, but *in themselves* not sufficient. At least they weren't for me.

In a day of instant coffee and the worship of convenience, our generation craves quick and easy spiritual formulas. But the Bible does not teach that we can be holy in a hurry. Biblical principles must be consistently applied before there is measurable spiritual progress.

We conquer those secret sins only as our thought patterns are changed by the Word of God. Every temptation comes to us via our thoughts. These must be replaced by wholesome thoughts, derived from the Word of God. This is basic to proving Christ's power in our lives. Paul says, "And do not be conformed to this world but be transformed by the renewing of your mind, that you may prove what the will of God is, that which is good and acceptable and perfect" (Romans 12:12, NASB*).

The difference between worldliness and godliness is a renewed mind. Your mind shapes your life. The Scriptures teach, "For as he thinks within himself, so he is" (Proverbs 23:7). The adage puts it succinctly: You aren't what you think you are; but what you think, you are!

Suppose we could flash all the thoughts you had last week on a giant screen. (I'm glad we can't. Agree?) Within minutes we'd know how you are doing spiritually. Your thoughts not only shape your life, they are your life.

A man recently released from prison was having difficulty adjusting to his freedom. He tried this experiment: he took a glass bottle with a distinct shape and crammed it full of wires, some small, some large. After some time had passed he smashed the bottle with a hammer. The result? Most of the wires retained the shape of the bottle. Those wires had to be straightened out one by one.

The man had established his point; it is possible to be free and still retain the traits of bondage. Even though a man is liberated, he must adjust to his freedom and carefully dismantle the habits of the past.

All believers are legally free in Christ but can still be enslaved by the fantasies of the flesh and the vices of the world. We can yield, surrender, and "pray through." But our minds will revert to familiar territory as soon as our experience wears thin. We must outline specific strategy for experiencing the freedom we have in Christ. We must accept the victory that already is legally ours.

---

*Unless noted otherwise, Scripture verses in this chapter are from the *New American Standard Bible*.

Is this really possible? Yes. But not without locking horns with wicked spiritual forces. Read carefully Paul's words. "For though we walk in the flesh, we do not war according to the flesh, for the weapons of our warfare are not of the flesh, but divinely powerful for the destruction of fortresses. We are destroying speculations and every lofty thing raised up against the knowledge of God, and *we are taking every thought captive to the obedience of Christ*" (2 Corinthians 10:3-5; italics added).

We have the spiritual artillery needed to destroy the fortresses of the mind. Vain reasonings, powerful imaginations, and perverted attitudes can be routed. We have the spiritual equipment to track down every thought and make it captive to Christ.

Specifically, how can we do this? To begin, we must learn to discern the difference between the thought patterns of the world and those of God. "How blessed is the man who does not walk in the counsel of the wicked, nor stand in the path of sinners, nor sit in the seat of scoffers" (Psalm 1:1).

David warns against receiving advice from the world. As Christians we have been slow to take his warning seriously. Often we adopt the values of the world under the guise of realism. A church member can be in love with money. He dreams about it, hankers after it, and is niggardly in his giving. He justifies his preoccupation with money by saying, "A person has to live." Without realizing it, he is taking his cue from the world. He is worldly to the core.

Other thought patterns are less subtle: pride, lust, anger, bitterness, and worry. We must take inventory of our thoughts and ask, Where did this thought originate? Blessed is the Christian who can clearly distinguish between thoughts that are from the world and those that are from God.

The first step in housecleaning our minds is to identify specifically the thoughts that must be swept out. Make a list of these sinful imaginations, then isolate the three that are the most troubling. You'll need this list if you want to have the furniture in your mind replaced, piece by piece.

Next, be prepared for the discipline of spiritual warfare. The world, the flesh, and the devil do not surrender without a struggle. The person who is blessed by God is one whose "delight is in the law of the Lord; and in his law doth he meditate day and night" (Psalm 1:2 KJV).

Sometimes we are told, "We are in a sprirtual battle. As soldiers of the cross we must be disciplined; we must put effort and sacrifice into the Christian life." Then, perhaps a week later another Christian appears to say just the opposite. "I was working too hard at being a Christian; God showed me that I must just hang loose—rest in the Lord."

Though these viewpoints appear contradictory, they really are not. *Only a Christian who is disciplined in the Word of God can rest in the Lord.* Yes, we must cease our striving and learn to relax in the confidence that God is equal to every situation. But a lazy, undisciplined Christian cannot do this;

he falls apart at the seams when tragedy strikes. The believer who is like a tree planted by the rivers of water is one who meditates in the law of God every free moment; his thoughts turn to the Word of God like steel to a magnet.

Declaring war on your thought life means that you must set aside time every morning to begin your offensive attack. I suggest twenty minutes as a minimum. Meditation in the Scriptures requires effort; nothing worth having can be achieved without exertion.

You've heard the cliche "A chapter a day keeps the devil away." Don't believe it. You can read a chapter with your mind on tomorrow's business deal or with a heart full of revenge. Real meditation requires quality time. We must assimilate a passage and give it our unhurried attention.

Third, you must be prepared to memorize the Word of God. "Thy word I have treasured in my heart, that I may not sin against Thee" (Psalm 119:11). Rather than memorize verses at random, take your list of troublesome thought patterns and find verses of Scripture that speak directly.

Memorize these verses so that you have them at your fingertips during the day. You'll need them. These are passages that God will use to demolish the present strongholds of your mind and construct a new edifice.

Here is how these verses can be used. First, prepare your mind *before* the temptation comes. Suppose your boss habitually irritates you. An hour after you arrive at work you wish you could scream. Don't wait until your boss shouts at you before you decide how you will respond. If so, you'll probably react in anger. Use the Word of God in anticipation. During your time with God in the morning, recite the verses you have memorized and claim Christ's victory *before* your boss blows his fuse.

If you wait until temptation comes to decide how you will react, you've waited too long. Choose beforehand to claim God's promises for whatever circumstances you expect to encounter.

Learn to obey the first promptings of the Holy Spirit. If you are tempted to enjoy a sensual fantasy, deal with those thoughts immediately. Each of us knows when we let our minds skip across that invisible line into forbidden territory. The moment we do so, we sense that we are violating the purity that the Holy Spirit desires. That is the moment to say, "I reject these thoughts in the name of the Lord Jesus," and then quote the passages of Scripture you have learned for that temptation. Undoubtedly, you will often fail. But with time, your sensitivity to the Holy Spirit will develop.

Use temptation as an alarm system—a signal to give praise to God. If, for example, you fear cancer, stop yourself short when this fear comes and give praise to God. Quote Romans 8:35-39 or read Psalm (e.g. 103, 144,145). Then thank God for all the blessings you have in Christ. Thank Him for forgiveness, for His sovereignty, power, and love. In this way, your stumbling block will be changed into a stepping stone. You'll be praising rather than pouting.

Whenever necessary, deal directly with Satan. Even if you consistently apply these suggestions, certain insidious thoughts may dart right back into your mind. For example, you may be filled with resentment. You reject those feelings in the name of the Lord Jesus; you even use Scripture. But angry thoughts force themselves upon you uninvited. The origin of such thoughts is no longer merely your sinful nature but demonic forces.

How do we confront these powers? We follow Christ's example who commanded, "Begone, Satan, for it is written. . . ." Use this formula (out loud if you are alone) and command him to depart on the basis of the Scripture you have claimed. Of course, shouting a verse of Scripture at demonic powers does not make them cringe (in the temptation of Christ, Satan retorted with a verse of his own). The power of the Word of God is unleashed when we bring ourselves under its authority.

God has given believers the right to deal with demonic forces, as long as the believers are under God's authority. To put it simply, only those who are *under* authority can *exercise* authority. Satan and his forces must flee when confronted with the bold use of biblical truth by a yielded child of the living God. So don't be afraid to confront satanic forces directly when you are wrestling with those sinister thoughts that refuse to exit.

How long does it take for our minds to be renewed? That depends. Some Christians who apply these principles recognize a noticeable difference within a week. Others, however, are steeped in decades of sin. For them it might take as long as thirty days before they can say, "I'm free!" And, of course, no one reaches perfection. The more we meditate on the Word, the more clearly we see new areas of our lives that need to be changed. Subtle motives often surface only after long exposure to the light of God's Word.

A homosexual who was freed from his life-style by using the above suggestions confessed that he often lapsed back into his former thought patterns before the strongholds of his mind capitulated to the power of Christ. "But now," he said, "when I think the thoughts I used to think, I get sick to my stomach." He is proof of what God can do in the life of anyone who persistently meditates in the Word of God and applies it directly to areas of spiritual conflict.

I'm convinced that Christ intended us to be free from mental bondage. His Word provides the resources to make our thoughts captive to the obedience of Christ. We can be free indeed.

19

Appendix 1

Pastors Who Have Served Moody Church

Founder: Dwight Lyman Moody 1864
    No regular pastor 1864–1866

Illinois Street Independent Church

    J. H. Harwood 1866–1869
    No regular pastor 1869–1871

North Side Tabernacle

    No regular pastor 1871–1876

Chicago Avenue Church

    William J. Erdman 1876–1878
    Charles M. Morton 1878–1879
    George C. Needham 1879–1881
    No regular pastor 1881–1885
    Charles F. Goss 1885–1890
    Charles A. Blanchard 1891–1893
    Reuben A. Torrey 1894–1906
    A. C. Dixon 1906–1911
    E. Y. Woolley (Acting) 1911–1915

Moody Tabernacle

> Paul Rader 1915–1921
> H. D. Campbell (Acting) 1922–1922

Moody Memorial Church

> P. W. Philpott 1922–1929
> H. A. Ironside 1930–1948
> H. A. Hermansen (Acting) 1948–1950
> S. Franklin Logsdon 1951–1952
> Alan Redpath 1953–1962
> No regular pastor 1962–1966
> George Sweeting 1966–1971
> Warren Wiersbe 1971–1978
> Erwin Lutzer 1980–

20

Appendix 2

The Moody Church Staff, November 1985

Erwin W. Lutzer, Senior Pastor
Bruce W. Jones, Associate Pastor
Grant M. Anderson, Christian Education Administrator
Paul S. Craig, Visitation Pastor
Gerald H. Edmonds, Minister of Music
David B. Craig, Minister of Youth
Matthew B. Heard, Minister of Singles and Evangelism
Dan Ward, Office Manager
Jim Guidone, Building Superintendent
John Persson, Camp Director
Dorothy Samorajski, Early Childhood Center Director
Warren Filkin, Associate Pastor Emeritus

1985 EXECUTIVE COMMITTEE MEMBERS

Elders

Dahlstrom, Richard	'91
Elsen, John	'91
Gustavson, E. Brandt	'88
Hayward, Charles	'90
Johnson, Carl	'88
Krumlin, Alfred	'88
Lahikainen, Ray	'88

Treasurer
    Lowman, Rex   '90
Assistant Treasurer
    Brockfield, Robert   '86
Director of Ushers
    Buske, Stan   '86
Assistant Director of Ushers
    Payne, Peter   '86
Clerk
    Cady, George   '86
Assistant Clerk
    Helstad, Wallace   '86
Director of Sunday School
    Karnath, Richard   '86
Ass't Director of Sunday School
    Helstad, Wallace   '86

Moody Press, a ministry of the Moody Bible Institute, is designed for education, evangelization, and edification. If we may assist you in knowing more about Christ and the Christian life, please write us without obligation: Moody Press, c/o MLM, Chicago, Illinois 60610.